Pursuit of ~~HAPPINESS~~ ASSETS

Pursuit of ~~HAPPINESS~~ ASSETS

KENNETH K. BOTWE

Copyright © 2019 Kenneth Botwe

ALL RIGHTS RESERVED.

No part of this book may be reproduced or transmitted in any form without permission in writing from the author. For information, please contact:

Kenko Publishing Corporation

8245 Mills Rd Houston Texas 77064

281-901-0158

www.DeviseWealth.com

www.Academy.DeviseWealth.com

Email: Info@DeviseWealth.com

Facebook Group: DeviseWealthMastermind

Twitter: @KennethBotwe

YouTube: KennethBotwe

LinkedIn: Ken Botwe

Facebook: Ken Botwe

Instagram: KenBotwe

Pinterest: KenBotwe

OTHER BOOKS BY KENNETH BOTWE

DEDICATION

This book is dedicated to Akua and Kwame. Thank you for complying with the proper discipline and guidance that our family bestowed upon you. Greatness awaits you both. Special gratitude to my team for assisting me in executing my vision of wealth creation education for the masses.

To my current and future students, I promise to stay relentless in the quest to help you transform your life and pursue assets.

TABLE OF CONTENTS

Introduction	**1**
SECTION I - Asset Power Moves: Why and How?	**5**
CHAPTER 1: Own and Control Resources	**7**
Tangible Assets	8
Intangible Assets	13
Sharpen Your Wealth Building Skills	17
OPR and OPM	20
CHAPTER 2: Money Generation	**27**
Lending	28
Creativity	37
Leverage Your Ability	40
CHAPTER 3: True Independence	**47**
Wealth	48
Health	51
Connection and Security	53
Controlling Your Destiny	55
Help Others	58
SECTION II - Asset Power Moves: When and How?	**61**
CHAPTER 4: Pursue Assets now	**63**
Mindset	63
Devise a Wealth Plan	65
Implement your plan	68
Evaluate and Make Adjustments	69
CHAPTER 5: Long Live Assets after Your Death	**71**
Asset Protection	72

Probate Avoidance and Anonymity	75
CHAPTER 6: Teach Your Children to Pursue Assets Early	**81**
The Approach	82
Teach Asset and Close Wealth Gap	83
It's About Your Legacy	86

SECTION III - Asset Power Moves: What and How? — 89

CHAPTER 7: Real Estate Above and Below Ground	**91**
Single Family One to Four Units	92
Multifamily Five Units or More	93
CHAPTER 8 - Turn-key & Strategic Business Alliances	**101**
Systems	101
Networking	104
CHAPTER 9: Stocks & Bonds Diversification	**107**
The Stock Market	108
Buying Debt AKA Bonds	111
Mutual funds	112

SECTION IV - Asset Power Moves: Where and How? — 113

CHAPTER 10: Opportunities in Your Region	**115**
Regionless Pursuit	115
Region Specific Opportunities	117
CHAPTER 11: Global Reach through Consulting	**121**
Caribbean Islands & South America	122
54 Countries of Africa	123
Asia	125
CHAPTER 12: Wherever technology reaches	**127**
Communications	128
Data Mining	129
Cloud Computing	130

SECTION V - Asset Power Moves: Who and How? — 133

CHAPTER 13 - Leadership	**135**

The Leader	136
The Vision	138
The Mission	138
CHAPTER 14 - Experienced Key Partners	**141**
Real Estate Broker/Agent	142
Corporate Attorney	142
Business & Tax Accountant	144
Other Key Partners	145
CHAPTER 15: A Team That Embodies Your Vision	**147**
Managers	147
The Workforce	148
Affiliates	151

Conclusion *153*

Other Publications & Educational Materials by the Author **156**

This book is intended to be used as a reference and readers must do their own independent verification. The author or the publisher is not rendering any legal, financial, tax, real estate or business advice and disclaim any personal liability from the content within. Care was used in the preparation of this document however, the author and publisher assume no responsibility for any errors herein.

INTRODUCTION

The universe is alive. It consistently produces and eliminates. A life that is created has a natural duty to survive or depart. This embodies a true sense of the phrase "survival of the fittest." As you may know, many of the universe creation do not make it. Those that persevere are endowed with the right to life. If you know what life is worth, you will not accept it without freedom, because the quality of life is not sustainable without liberty.

Happiness, on the other hand, is internal. I submit to you that happiness is self-made. It is limited to just you and no one else. Therefore it has no value. Families cannot use happiness to pay for shelter, food, clothing, and other basic necessities of life. In your community, it cannot provide safety and security or recreational amenities. Nations cannot operate and thrive or defend itself with happiness.

If the world was content with happiness, why has there been war consistently somewhere since the beginning of times? Surely these conflicts have never been about happiness. Happiness is only a feeling. It can emerge and vanish as you yearn for more, or conditions that surrounds it changes. Due to its limitation and volatility, the desire for happiness should not be a primary or secondary aim of anyone. Do not engage in the pursuit of happiness.

You should pursue assets instead. That's right; focus on solid tangible and intangible assets. It can cure all the challenges mentioned above that happiness cannot. As you accumulate assets, construct an adequate protection mechanism to ensure its survival. Through these actions, sustainable families, communities, and nations are built.

Asset is a useful or valuable property that can be owned. It is power and the ability to act in a particular way. Asset is also the capacity to direct or influence the behavior of others or the course of events. Dr. Martin Luther King said, "Power without love is reckless and abusive, and love without power is sentimental and anemic. Power at its best is love implementing the demands of justice, and justice at its best is power correcting everything that stands against love." As you read through the 5 W's and H in the 5 subsequent sections titled Asset Power Moves, remember that I'm referring to power with love, and implementing the demands of justice. If ever there's a question in your mind, let this serve as the yardstick for dealing with humanity.

An asset has a value that can be traded for goods and services. It is defined as anything or anyone that can be used as a resource to generate income. Asset is considered a key resource in paying debts and meeting certain commitments because asset has economic value that can be converted into present and future cash. Whether it's a job, an inheritance, or attained through your efforts with a team, of course, asset is necessary.

Although it's all good, my interest is positioning the willing for the latter. This is the premise of the project, and all that unfolds are intended to be used for that purpose. When going after resources, be principled, and never commit human rights violations. Always fairly compensate all original owners or workers in accordance with fair and prior agreements. I emphasize being fair because unfairness anywhere by nature will eventually correct itself through evolution or revolution.

Going forth and accumulating or creating assets the right way is meaningless if you ignore the violations of others, therefore defend the defenseless. The universe bends towards justice, so your race, religion, language, and culture will not make a difference. Your assets will grow and eventually outlive you, making it transgenerational. You will enjoy wealth and prosperity regardless of where you originated or migrated from on the planet.

What are these assets that I speak of, you may ask? The answers will emerge throughout the 5 sections of this publication. You will benefit from the detailed results of the examination into why we should pursue assets. An analysis of when is the right time to engage in your pursuit will be conducted. Lastly, you'll have the insight to scan wherever you are for asset opportunities properly. All types of asset solutions are explored throughout these chapters, and it includes how to pursue them, with or without cash. I hope this useful publication inspires you to make power moves to financial freedom through assets.

SECTION I

Asset Power Moves: Why and How?

There are many reasons to pursue assets and none is wrong if done ethically. Ask yourself and uncover your own unique reasons. When you reach the level of determining why you should pursue assets, all answers should be based on personal ambitions, both now and in terms of legacy. The entire process of asset pursuit makes no sense unless you know why you're doing it. It is a matter of personal journey. No answer is incorrect as long as it has elements of a burning desire to do it.

You must pursue assets legally. Although money is the primary way to attain assets, other resources such as your skill, talents, gifts, training, experience and creativity can be just as valuable to the process. Take inventory of who you are. Even if you possess no resources that can be leveraged to attain assets, the fact that you are alive and healthy may be all you need. With a strong will, you'll find a way. Anyone can be trained to do anything. Construct a roadmap of how to reach your goal. It does not have to be perfect as adjustments can be made down the line.

In the next few chapters, you're going to discover the answers to the questions why and how to pursue assets. You'll go beyond the basics, and learn prime reasons why it's worthwhile to pursue assets and how to build the framework for it. We'll dive even deeper into what gains can be expected and the importance of proper education in assets. If properly understood, this section will enlighten you in developing your own unique justification for asset pursuit, and the action plan to pull it off.

CHAPTER ONE:

Own and Control Resources

Although the basic reason is survival, one of the chief reasons why people pursue assets is to own and control resources. Since it is a matter of long-term survival, many commit unspeakable crimes to attain and maintain it. While many use deceit, some pursue it with dignity. Others are indifferent, and behave as though their interest at the moment is dormant. This behavior may be as a result of not knowing the difference between assets and liabilities. Look at it this way; if it makes you money, it's an asset. If it cost you money, it's a liability.

It seems many just never feel as if it is possible for them to own and control resources. Consequently, they join the rat race without an exit plan and teach their children to do the same. My goal is to provoke a mindset shift so that their fair share does not continue to go to the greedy. It is my hope that you create and accumulate your assets to a point where you become an employer and no longer an employee. All of it can be done the rights way. Perpetrating unethical and illegal actions to acquire assets should be avoided at all cost.

Remember, the universe bends towards justice. Therefore, you reap what you sow. All those who have violated are paying or will one day pay the ultimate price. With that being said, let's take a closer look into some assets. Basically, if it can be converted into revenue, it's an asset. There are two types of assets. One is tangible and the other, intangible.

Tangible Assets

Tangible assets are resources with a physical existence one can touch, feel, and see. Examples of tangible assets include land and bodies of water such as ocean, rivers, and lakes. In densely populated cities, air space is also regarded that way. In fact, some have a hefty price. We will talk more about air space in a bit later. Real estate structures and physical businesses are also classified as tangibles as well as machinery, money, and inventory of all types.

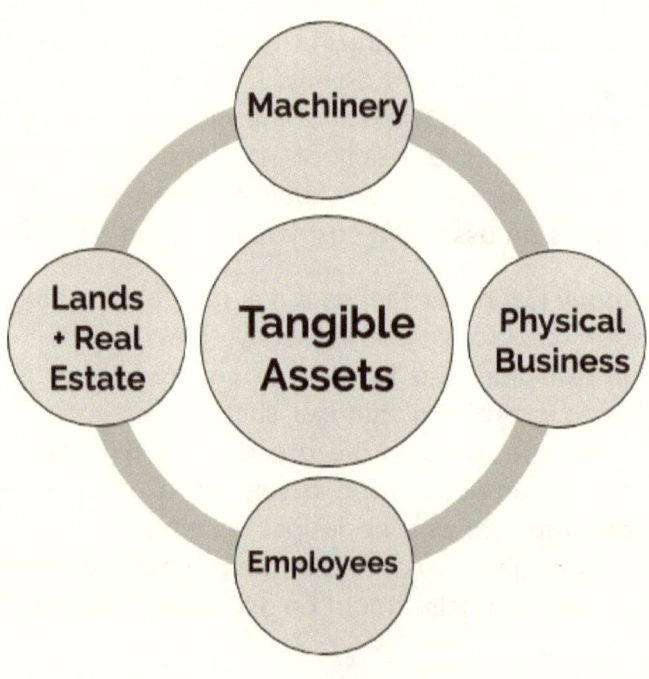

Land is used to produce agriculture, an essential food, and product source that is necessary for the sustainability of life. It is also used for the construction of commercial and residential buildings as well as forestry. Underneath the surface of land lies many useful deposits of water and fossils. Above it is air space, the venue that some say will one day become the primary mode of transportation for the masses. For now, land surface is by far the number one method of transportation.

Even though land is finite, much of its resources are yet to be unearthed. The nature of real property, such as land is that it appreciates when it is developed.

According to fortune.com, real estate advisor company Savills has estimated the global land at $227 trillion. That is ever-increasing number will continue to rise as more developments come into existence. Underneath its surface lies water, minerals, and fossil fuels, both discovered and yet to be discovered.

On our planet, land only consists of 29% while the remainder is all water. This water in the form of ocean is a mega source of the global economy as it is used for fishing, tourism, water sports, and transportation worldwide. Shorelines all over the world are used to build beachfront properties like hotels, casino, amusement parks, restaurants, shops, homes, and much more. These dwellings are a major assets for the tourism industry.

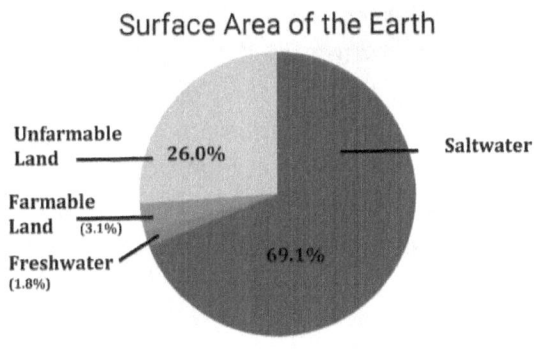

Fishing for the most part and transportation via water are possible partly because of our seas, rivers, and lakes. These days, humans tend to construct artificial versions of virtually anything. Some are useful, while others may be to our detriment. Fishing farms are no exception, and many are found all over the world. One way to correct commercial fisheries that do not follow best practices is not to patronize them.

On a larger scale, constructions such as the Panama and Suez canals are just a couple of examples that have made international trade more convenient. They make international water transportation shorter and cheaper because the two named canals joins the Atlantic - Pacific Oceans and Mediterranean - Red Sea, respectively. Let's hope that no environmental responsibilities were ignored during these massive constructions.

The value of our ocean is estimated at $24 trillion according to world wildlife. Offshore drilling is yet another integral part of overall oil production, and it's not even included in the previous estimate. Furthermore, many projects are yet to be initiated in the vast ocean of ours. Rivers and lakes serves a similar purpose as oceans in terms of fishing and water sports but on a much smaller, yet important scale.

Air space is indeed an asset as well, especially in populated cities around the world. It too can be sold for substantial amount of money.

One example is the vertical rights sale of Christ Church in New York. Apparently, the owners of that building sold its air space rights for over $30 million. I'm quite sure; this is not an isolated case. Many in especially congested cities have a need to construct buildings that are wider at the top than at the base. In such cases, a builder may purchase air space of an adjacent shorter building and expand its building right over it.

Real estate structures are constructed over land or water and sometimes extended horizontally in the air. It can be used for commercial or residential purposes. It can also be sold or leased. An expectation based on historical facts is that it usually appreciates in value over time.

Also, most nation's tax codes allow depreciation deductions for a number of years ranging from twenty-five to thirty years. Such allowance is twenty-seven and a half years in the United States.

This deduction is due to the assertion that buildings will deteriorate over time and therefore allowance is granted for repairs and upkeep. Real estate will be covered extensively in chapter 7 as it is a realistic and major asset for the ordinary man or woman to pursue.

Physical businesses are classified into three main types.

The first type is services based. It provides intangibles such as professional training, skill, education, expertise, and things that are not provided in the physical form. Online training, delivery, eldercare, real estate brokerage, dry-cleaning, daycare, personal fitness trainer, lawyer, insurance agent, doctor, mechanic, hair stylist, technician, and scientist are just a few examples of businesses based on service.

The second type is product based and consist of buying at wholesale and selling at retail prices. All products that fall into this category are usually purchased and sold without any modifications. Examples of product-based businesses are online stores, grocery shops, boutiques, furniture stores, pharmacies, apparel shopping centers, mobile phone kiosk, convenient stops, and car dealerships, etc.

The third type is manufacturing based. This type of business transform products and sell them as either wholesale or retail. They typically operate out of a factory or laboratory and use a combination of raw material and other items to produce a new product for sale.

Pharmaceutical companies, shipbuilders, arts & craft makers, chemical laboratories, agriculture manufacturing, automobile makers, clothing factories, aircraft makers, and home builders are just a few examples of manufacturing companies.

Machinery for infrastructure, agriculture, defense, safety, travel, health, communications, exploration, and convenience on land, air, and water are all resources necessary to develop a nation. These machines are only manufactured in a few privileged countries; thus opportunities to position such plants, assemblies, laboratories and factories in countries of scarcity are currently abundant.

Money is used as a medium of exchange between people and businesses all over the world. It solves the problem of attaining needed goods and services. Money can be used as a solution to many challenges people and nations face today. Nearly all nations have their own money in the form of currency.

The dinar, a Kuwaiti currency, is regarded as the strongest at the time of this writing in 2019, where 1 dinar equals 3 dollars. Like the dollar, several other nations use dinar. Among them is Bahrain, which is number two, by the way, Jordan which sits at number four, and several other countries in the Persian Gulf. The American dollar has the number nine spot. According to the Central Intelligence Agency, there is approximately $80 trillion circulating globally.

TOP 10 - World Currencies (2019)
No.1 – Kuwait Dinar (1 KWD = 3.29 USD) ...
No.2 – Bahraini Dinar (2.65 USD) ...
No.3 – Oman Rial (2.60 USD) ...
No.4 – Jordan Dinar (1.41 USD) ...
No.5 – British Pound Sterling (1.26 USD) ...
No.6 – Cayman Islands Dollar (1.20 USD) ...
No.7 – European Euro (1.14 USD)
No.8 – Swiss Franc (1.04 USD)
No.9 – US Dollar (1.00 USD)
No.10 – Canadian Dollar (.075 USD)

Inventory of all types and purpose are kept for resale and use across all sectors of the economy and all industries in the world. By nature, people are consumers of inventory from food source to other products.

Some inventory, such as fresh food has a shelf life of a few hours, and others such as homes, a few decades provided they are well maintained. They are both nonetheless tangible assets as there are many others. Frankly, the list is too extensive to name. If it can be prepared and sold at a later time, consider it an inventory and such inventory is an asset.

Intangible Assets

Intangible assets do not have a physical existence. Examples of intangible assets include investment such as stocks and bonds.

A mere evidence of owning these types of securities is the receipt. Your skill and talent are an asset if it is useful to relatively many people. Other examples of intangible assets are patents, brand, copyright, trademark, and trade secrets. Let's take a closer look at each one these intangible assets.

To simplify its description, a stock is a smaller share of a company. In other words, when a corporation divides its shares and issues ownership to others, it is called stocks. It is usually sold but can also be distributed as compensation or incentive to its executives. Companies issue and sell shares as a way to raise money internally without applying for a loan. When the company does well on the stock market or if more people demand to buy that particular stock, the value of the share rises. The value falls when the opposite occurs. The transaction process is known as trading. Once upon a time, trading of stocks was done physically. This dynamic has since been automated and takes place around the clock, although the markets themselves have operating hours.

Pursuit of ~~Happiness~~ Assets

Governments need money to run nations in terms of legislation, defense, infrastructure, safety, schools, security, and other essential areas of human activity. They collect taxes to help fund the respective institutions, but overuse causes shortages. They need to borrow money.

The world banks are a destination for loans, but sometimes nations lend from its citizens. In this scenario, they issue bonds or a certificate in exchange for a loan from the general public and institutions. There is a maturity date for the value of the bond to be repaid plus a predetermined interest rate. In a nutshell, people who lend money to governments do so in the form of receiving a bond certificate. These receipts are issued with all terms stipulated.

There are many other forms of securities, like stocks and bonds and commodities like wheat and oil. A simple way to differentiate them is long term and short-term investment assets, respectively. Among them are mutual funds, annuities, futures, and options, to name a few. Mutual funds are an investment where a pool of money is invested by a firm strategically on the people's behalf. Annuities are paid by insurance companies and other firms periodically to investors based on a contract. Futures is an agreement between a firm and an investor to buy or sell on a future date at a predetermined price. An investment type where you have the right but are not obligated to buy or sell is known as options.

Skill is a high degree of competence. People with skills cannot be replaced by just anyone. That makes them an asset. The question becomes, are you using your skill optimally?

A simple investigation can reveal the answer to propel you to the right utilization of your skill. Refrain from being complacent and be certain instead. Like skill, talent is also an asset, except it is natural. A talented person may not require any formal training to excel in what they do.

Their ability comes from a habit. When one is gifted, he or she has high-performance capabilities in a variety of areas. When harnessed properly, a gifted person can be a huge asset and excel far beyond others. Whether its academia, corporate, sports, arts, or another area, skill, talent, and gift are all regarded as an intangible asset.

Patent rights are granted to inventors in exchange for public disclosure by the patent office. To get a patent right, there must not be a prior patent of the same type on file. It also gives the owner the exclusive rights for a number of years where others cannot make, use, or sell the invention. Prior to the year 1790 and before records of inventor's race were kept, thousands of slave inventors were not credited. While working as an Assistant United States Patent Officer, Henry E. Baker, a Harvard Law School Graduate, dedicated his life to searching and revealing black inventors.

He wrote to lawyers all across the United States with one purpose in mind. He asked the lawyers to identify any black inventors they may have filed a patent for. As a result, he uncovered and published four massive volumes of black inventions he had examined. Much of these patents are tremendous intangible assets went to the owners of the slaves since slaves were not allowed to own anything.

Brand is a marketing symbol, mark, name, or product that distinguishes it from others. When branding is done correctly, it takes a life of its own and remains very distinctive. Amazon is currently the world's most valuable brand. The owner of Amazon is Jeff Bezos, and he is currently the richest man in the world at a net worth of $139.8 billion.

Copyright is an exclusive legal right that grants the originator the determination of conditions under which his or her work may be used.

One's work, such as film, music, and publications, can all be copyrighted. This action prevents people from unauthorized use or sale. It is worth to note that even an unpublished work can be copyrighted for protection. The universal symbol for copyright is ©. Many also simply put the word copyright in parenthesis.

Trademark is a recognizable word, name, symbol, or design used to identify and distinguish products or services and to indicate its source. The universal symbol for a registered trademark is® while the unregistered trademark is ™. The difference between the two is that unregistered trademark is not legally granted by a statute; however, the owner has legal right within the region in which they operate.

A trade secret is a technique, process, or formula used by a company that is not known by others. This type of practice usually gives a business a competitive advantage over others.

Good trade secrets are valuable, and all efforts to maintain its secrecy should be a company's policy. All the above-mentioned intangible assets are all intellectual properties. Even a valuable idea is also considered as such and therefore must be properly guarded.

If you feel that you cannot own and control any of the resources mentioned above, you are not alone. Many people do not have that capability by themselves. Owning and controlling resources in any meaningful way requires education and creativity for identifying opportunities, as well as forming teams and alliances for seizing them.

Sharpen Your Wealth Building Skills

Make continued learning an integral part of your journey by sharpening your wealth building skills. Be prepared to re-educate yourself on personal finance as a whole with a focus on business, real estate, and investments. I'm sorry, but what most people learned in the traditional school setting is designed for an employee. The proper education I'm referencing is for people who through assets, can become employers. This book will show you how. Supplemental publications are also referenced to help you. A real attempt should be made to learn more about eliminating bad debt, including your mortgage, maintaining great credit, using leverage, asset protection, and building wealth systems. It is wise to learn from successful people that are reputable and experienced, such as myself. We'll cover more on these topics throughout this book.

Besides reading this book, make it a personal policy to read and view all of my other publications and content such as books, e-books, YouTube videos, blogs, webinars, e-Courses, podcast, and other guest appearances, and join my FREE Facebook group (Devise Wealth Mastermind) to get the best we have to offer. When you reach the right level of understanding, take one step further by reaching out to me for mentorship or coaching. This specially tailored one on one session will help you take your wealth building to a higher level. Essential success leaves clues, but this one should be deliberate to cut the learning curve.

Please understand that everyone can learn to eliminate all bad debt, including your house. In fact, wealth building is done so much faster when you eliminate all your bad debt first. Becoming totally bad debt free is not a myth, it is very much a reality that can happen if you learn how and execute the methods I teach. If you have a house, let me show you how to pay it off in five years. Yes, that's right. You can pay off your mortgage in five years using the resources you already have at your disposal. With at least a combined income of fifty thousand, if you have children, and forty thousand with no kids, I can help you accomplish that. Essentially regardless of your income, if you were able to buy a house, I can teach you to pay it off in 5 to 7 years.

If you don't have a house, you need one, especially if you're paying rent to a landlord. To build wealth from the bottom, having a paid off house will expedite the process much to your delight. Many methods can be used to begin the wealth process way before the house is paid off. My FREE YouTube video, as well as my e-course, will illustrate how to get one and pay it off in five years. This is not magic; it's a system. It's scientific, and it works every time if you follow it. The benefits of having 100% ownership of the equity in your home are too many to list. Utilization of the benefits goes as far as your vision. Getting yourself out of credit cards trouble is just part of the process. Learn about having great credit and how it will help you leverage resources to enrich yourself.

If you do not have a credit score of at least 800 and a credit line of at least a quarter million dollars, my system will teach you that as well. So whether you have no credit, bad, fair, or good credit, your aim should be to increase it to a great credit. For those that do not have credit at all, you are covered, my videos teaches you how to establish credit and build it to the same 800 credit score or higher within a year and a substantial credit line of at least two hundred and fifty thousand dollars. You should also make it a priority to learn how to save money short term. The result will be saved money and a big credit line, two necessary ingredients for the recipe of wealth creation.

Other than an inheritance, a lotto, professional sports, entertainment, and executive level positions, or specialized profession such as doctors, etc., most people cannot build wealth without the acquisition of business assets or real estate. More videos are available, and it focuses on short term savings for assets. You'll learn how to allocate money for the purpose of buying assets. All you need is up to 30% of the funds as the remainder will come from a lender.

Your training will enable you to truly differentiate and say no to liabilities while welcoming assets into your life. If you don't own any assets, it time to begin. It must be, however, the right type of assets. When done correctly, your assets will increase in value over time. You're going to learn how to get tax benefits in the form of depreciation, interest deductions, and expense allowances. Most of all, your training will enable you to only acquire assets that will produce cash flow. Learn how to leverage what you have to get what you want.

OPR and OPM

In my previous book, Little Money Big Credit, I talked about a variety of systems that the wealthy use to get wealthier. Among them is the system of leveraging other people's resources or (OPR) and other people's money or OPM. Now, you may say if they're wealthy, why do they need other people's resources? The simple answer is they don't. They prefer it because they have a sound financial education. Besides knowing their own money can only go so far to match their high ambitions for wealth, the wealthy understand how to make every hundred dollars of investment go three times the distance of a poor person. They also know how to utilize people's expertize. In essence, this process is fundamental to the rich. They have mastered it, and would not dare do a deal without it.

The economic condition of the wealthy businessman is ripe for lending. It's imperative that you learn to do the same. When you do, they will give you at a minimum, seventy dollars for every thirty dollars that you have for real estate. They'll lend more for a sound business. This is other people's money or OPM. As your net worth increases, you'll qualify for an even better ratio until eventually, they'll say how much do you need?

We just mentioned money in terms of other's resources, but it stretches far beyond money. It can be other people's time, talent, expertise, and systems, to name a few. All of these resources can be utilized via hiring, contracting, or buying. The point is that you make things as easy as it can be by tapping into other people resources. Be mindful that money itself can all vanish, but sound assets will stand the test of time.

Learning and preparation is perhaps one of the biggest part of building wealth. That is why professional athletes study their opponent and train before their match. The same applies to wealth building. Besides understanding what they entail, some mindsets must be adopted during the learning phase of your journey. Have a mindset to minimize liabilities and maximize assets. Your financial affairs should be operated as if it were a business.

We have confidence in money when the economy is good. This is one of the reasons why currencies from countries with a thriving economy are valued higher than those without and vice versa. When an economy dives into a depression for an extended period, its currency will likely weaken. If attempts to remedy it involves printing too much money by the federal reserves, it will cause inflation and therefore further cause the money to be devalued. The takeaway is that money can come and go and your wealth should not be defined by how much money you have. Instead, money must be transformed into an income producing asset. Lastly, money should work for you, not you for money

Please understand that success in wealth creation is much easier with credit. When this factor is properly understood, it becomes a mindset that causes one to act in accordance with utilizing credit every chance they get. It's OPM (other people's money), and you can borrow much more of it than you have at your disposal. This is because the lender looks at your net worth and your cash on hand in the financial statement and will lend you significantly more than you have in cash. It makes absolutely no sense to use your own money to undertake a venture.

Credit is now more important than ever especially since money itself is no longer backed by precious metals in arguably the strongest nation in the world. Society has been catapulted into consuming at a higher rate, but the sad thing is that those that aren't financially literate consume to make others rich. When people suddenly begin to see the full picture, they are poised to make changes to the way they spend, especially when using credit. Know that credit is more powerful than money, and it should be used to acquire assets, not liabilities. When you leverage money and credit in wealth building, you'll go far.

Whenever something is used to maximize advantages, it is referred to as leverage. It entails using resources at your disposal to advance your agenda of building wealth. The resources could be a partnership venture, debt, systems of instruments, expertise, or other human resources. Essentially, if it can help you attain your goal of building wealth, its leverage. Leverage cuts into time, money, effort, and learning curve in financial matters. Everyone uses it, but not many know the proper application and ramification of leverage.

If you take 100% of your own money to purchase or finance a business, you have failed to use leverage. Likewise, manually doing something that can be done with a tool at much higher efficiency is the absence of leverage. Trying to do your own business taxes or draw your own legal documents when a competent professional can do it properly is negligence of leverage. More on leveraging education will be covered in chapter 2.

Keep in mind that things of value must be protected. Many of us are mandated to protect our homes, cars, and health with insurances. When you have something valuable, such as your life and other assets, the sentiment of protection should remain high on your radar. To put it another way, if you cannot afford to lose it, protect it. The question of asset protection is extremely important to those that aspire to build wealth and those that are already in progress.

It is a tragedy for anyone to work hard and build a valuable entity only to lose it to theft, lawsuit, damage, and so forth. Look at it this way; asset protection should be used to guard your assets tangible and intangible. Asset protection is also separating yourself from your wealth by incorporating. Although many know they should, a vast majority do it inadequately while a small group fails to take any measures at all. Make leverage and asset protection a priority in your business.

When a large portion of your hard-earned money is taxed, and you discover that others legally pay the least minimum to nothing at all, you should want to know why. Because taxes are taken before you are paid as employees, many don't feel the loss. 30% or more is taken so tactfully that people don't care enough to see if something can be done to remedy it. Others simply don't pay attention to how much tax liabilities is costing them.

I desire to let you know that tax code, in general, is written to allow tax breaks to people that provide jobs, housing, food, and energy. The breaks and deductions are so enormous that a company could end up paying absolutely nothing once they've taken advantage of all the tax savings allowed by law. Every effort should be made to unmask the tax code. Becoming a beneficiary of such savings cannot be far from anyone agenda, especially if building wealth is your primary goal.

It does not mean that you have to thoroughly understand it

after reading. Many just don't have the background required to gain full comprehension, however, your tax accountant should. A collaboration between your CPA and your business attorney will result in a tax savings strategy designed for your unique undertaking. There is no need to try and figure it out on your own and take chances that may result in a penalty. Use the expert professional of your team, specifically your corporate attorney and your CPA for the best tax strategy. I'm emphasizing this process because tax savings should not be strategize without a CPA and corporate attorney.

Furthermore, tax savings requires organization and proper documentation. When it comes to the subject of tax savings, it is better to take information from your certified public accountant and corporate lawyer. They are going to apply the tax code strategically as it pertains to the business that you wish to undertake.

I've seen so many people who simply lack the knowledge of how money is supposed to flow. Their financial statement tells me all I need to know. Money is an actor, and you are the director. In other words, money only goes where you direct it. The fact that you have total control must be properly understood so you can send it where it benefits you. Spending all your money on liabilities month in month out, and year in year out is not a mark of the financially astute. The person who knows money focuses rather on how to impregnate it to produce more.

Money has a definite direction of flow in terms of wealth building. It's called cash flow, and it should be flowing towards you, not away from you. Not getting it right means remaining trapped in a cycle that does not benefit you. Even worse, you can't get out of it. It is a shame how people are indoctrinated so well about the wrong management of money that there has to be a major mentality shift to break them out of it. Those that do break out, however, never go back. They gain clarity, and building wealth becomes a top priority. These people usually operate with such urgency in terms of financial education and undertaking.

Just like you protect your house and your car by locking it, do the same for all your other assets. In later chapters, I will teach you how to install protective mechanisms to shield you from scammers, thieves, and opportunist. Asset protection is a very important part of building wealth, and it must be done right from the start of your organization and during various stages as you grow. Having protection will give you the peace of mind you need to focus on wealth creation.

You even have to learn to evaluate results and determine which success is worth repeating. Don't get complacent after tasting the success of wealth accumulation for the first time. Keep going by repeating what has worked well. This time, however, do it in a bigger and in a greater fashion to increase the returns. It can be duplicated or expanded. It can even be diversified. Whatever it may be, however, it has to include the acquisition of larger assets. Learn how to use arbitrage to go after the best deal and ROI or return on investment.

Learning is an ongoing practice, and it never stops. Make it fun and enjoy every step of the process. It is important to have multiple streams of income, so even when one industry slows; others are booming.

Five should be the minimum number of different revenues that you generate from assets. Among the must include are offline products/services business, online products/services business or e-commerce, residential real estate, commercial real estate, and investments in paper assets

The pursuit of assets is about joining forces and resources like talent, money, skill, and experience. It's also about staying highly motivated in executing the overall vision and mission of the establishment that you formulate or join.

Please understand that it is sometimes better to be part of something big than being small all by yourself. A small portion of something big is better than a big portion of something small. Make this key wisdom part of your mindset when it comes to assets. Ultimately, put yourself in the position to own and control resources even if it's only a portion.

"You have little power over what's not yours." - *Zimbabwean proverb*

CHAPTER TWO:

Money Generation

Money Generation is another key factor as to why people pursue assets. In the genesis, access to capital can be a challenge. Where you start depends on your individual situation. For instance, someone that's unemployed and has no savings faces a different challenge than the person with a job and suitable reserved money. All the same, people with skill and experience can leverage it towards asset acquisition. Although many factors are at play, cash, credit, and skill are the front runners. Sometimes, it's a matter of using all three and other times; it takes even more. You must master the art of leveraging when it comes to money generation. Having the credit, for instance, is good, but leveraging it to acquire assets is better.

This holds true whether you are starting an asset such as a business or buying one. The fact remains, you must be able to generate money or its equivalent in order to pursue assets. That, in turn, becomes a money generator.

Anything that can be liquidated quickly into cash serves the same purpose.

Finding a path when it seems there's no way is a matter of being relentless in the pursuit.

Don't take no for an answer. Talent, experience, or whatever attributes you possess must be utilized to negotiate and do deals if you cannot get access to money using conventional methods.

Let's explore several ways to get the funds needed to begin asset acquisition. Leveraging money and credit is an important area that will be presented as well.

Lending

Lending is one of the smartest ways to secure funds needed to acquire an asset. Some conditions must be met for banks and other lenders to give you the money. Banks and creditors like for borrowers to have "skin in the game," meaning they will usually require you to have a down payment of your loan amount.

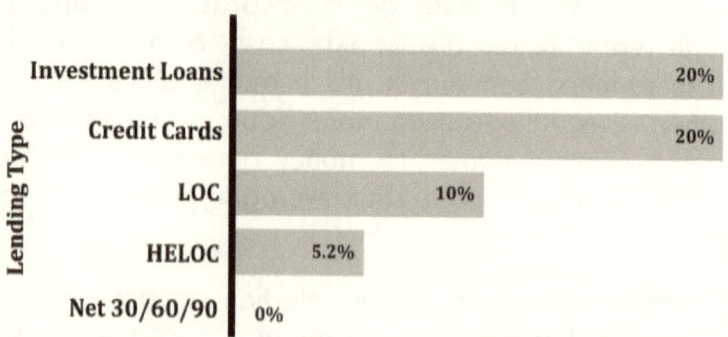

The amount differs with each asset and can range from 1% to as high as 50% although the average is 15%. Lending institutions are businesses, too, and they take calculated steps to minimize risk. They will verify that you have sufficient income source in proportion with the loan amount. Aside from down payment and closing cost, anyone seeking to borrow money must demonstrate creditworthiness. With your permission, a credit report will be ordered to see your history.

The major things that are examined are your Fair Isaac Corp's or FICO score, negative items such as collections, bankruptcies, liens, late payments, credit utilization, and finally debt-to-credit ratio. The average FICO score in America is 695. Please do not confuse credit score with FICO score as the two scores usually vary. FICO score is based on your borrowing capacity and ability to pay on time per terms of your loan or trade lines in general.

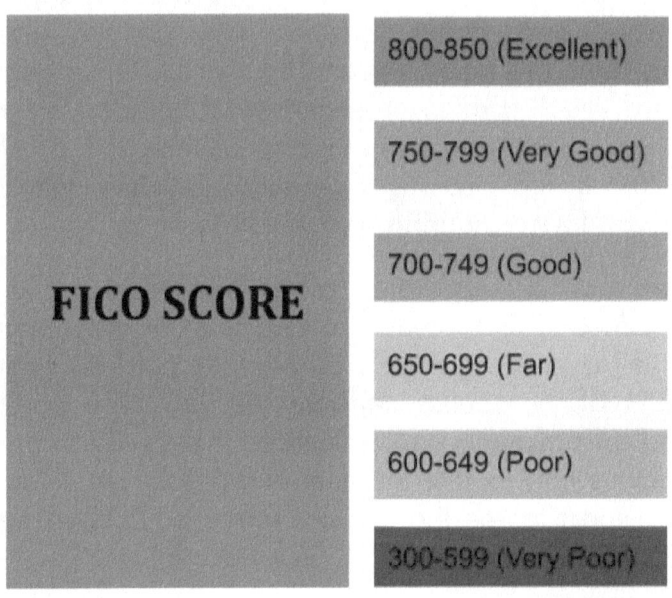

Collections indicate that the borrower failed to pay their debt per terms of the agreement. As a consequence, that debt was either sold to a collection agency or sent for assistance in exchange for a commission. Either way, having a collection on your credit report gives lenders a red flag about your repayment tendencies. If other indicators are good and you can cure the collection issue, lenders may reconsider. This process, however, takes time because most collection agencies will update information with credit reporting agencies once a week.

They may take up to thirty days to update per The Fair Credit Reporting Act, a United States federal legislation. Debt delinquencies that goes to the collection will remain on your credit report for seven years if it does not get resolved.

Bankruptcies are yet another discrepancy lenders frown upon. It tells a story of a borrower that discharged their debt instead of paying them. The banks don't want to risk their money to someone that discharges their debt. There are many types of bankruptcies and many reasons why people choose it. However, none are good for lending money. Once bankruptcy is reported, it will take seven to ten years before it is removed. Even if you change your mind and dismiss the proceeding, bankruptcy is reported as dismissed. Lenders still tend to penalize you for considering and initiating it.

Liens are usually a product of tax delinquency, judgment against someone that losses in a civil court or a contractor that feels as if they were not paid or partially paid for their work. Regardless of the source, lenders see you as a person that defaulted on payment. Like collection, there's sometimes hope if you move swiftly to cure the debt and get the lien lifted. If not, you can expect to see the lien on your credit report for seven whole years.

Late payments are inconvenient, annoying, and may prevent others from meeting their obligations. For example, a wholesaler may not supply a retailer if payments are late. Without retail, customers demand cannot be met. Employees can also be affected if payments are not received on time. To discourage untimely payments, business institutions report late payments to the credit bureaus. Having late payments on your credit can deter banks from lending you money, especially if it's more than 60 days late. It is better to make every effort to pay your bills on time.

Debt-to-credit ratio is a metric that shows your credit utilization. There are two reasons why you should care about this ratio. First, your credit score takes a hit when your debt-to-credit ratio exceeds 30%. In other words, your credit score begins to lose points. The higher your ratio, the more points you lose. Secondly, lenders tend to play it safe and refrain from lending to people with a high debt-to-credit ratio.

When you stay under the specified ratio, you essentially avoid a credit score decrease as well as the possibility of being denied credit.

As you begin your quest to accumulating assets, do it with fairness and integrity. Pay whomever you owe and demand that you are also paid when you are owed. Just as you can be reported negatively for discrepancies, you can also report your debtors. An example would be tenants if you own rental real estate and they fail to remit payment as due. Make every effort to make good on your obligations. More importantly, it is not wise to let a small problem grow into a bigger one. Take measures to correct small problems as they arise. You'll have less hassle along the way to owning assets.

There are various forms of credit lines that one can utilize for capital. Among some of the more practical ones are HELOC, LOC, credit card, and even vendor line of credit. The one chosen would depend on the options available to the borrower.

All lines of credit are not created equal. Some have lower variable interest rates, while others have a net 30. That simply means vendors must be paid within 30 days of the invoice date.

HELOC or Home equity line of credit may perhaps be an option for money generation. If lending is not possible and you've owned a home for several years, it should have increased in equity.

Consequently, this equity can be accessed. It grows when you have paid down your mortgage, or there is a rise in property value. This equity in itself is an asset that should not be allowed the sit idle. Instead, it should be used to generate the money needed as down payment for more asset acquisition. As you repay, you can use the HELOC again.

The strategy of utilizing equity in your home is important, but it should be used strictly to control more assets. Using it for liabilities will only exacerbate the "rat race" problem. Currently, the average interest rates in America for a home equity loan is 5.2%.

This rate is variable and changes with the market. Consider what interest you're already paying versus the current interest and future outlook to help you decide. When calculated carefully, this method can be used periodically to ascend towards your goal.

For example, a $400,000 home with a balance of $200,000 will yield a home equity loan of up to $140,000. This type of money can be used to leverage a $700,000 loan. In some places, you can buy a small apartment complex with that kind of money.

Beware, there is an average closing cost of 3% due at closing for a home equity loan. Evaluate interest rate difference plus closing cost carefully to make sure it is worth using this strategy.

Since the home itself serves as collateral, requirements for HELOC and home equity loans are relatively relaxed than other lines of credit. Liens and judgments however could be an obstacle and would need to be cured before a lender will grant you the line. It can never be overemphasized to take care of little things such as disputes and taxes before it becomes major and end up costing you more. The last note about HELOC and home equity loans is that you must have a mortgage in order to get it. Make every effort to purchase a home at an early age as opposed to renting an apartment. In this case, although your home is a liability, you can convert it into an asset. You cannot do that with renting from a landlord. Besides, you can "cut the cloth according to your size," meaning buy a house with a mortgage payment close to what you're already paying for an apartment.

Line of credit or LOC is also available as an option in money generation. Annual percentage rate or APR is variable based on the prime rate and is around 10% at the time of this writing. There is usually a small annual fee of approximately $25. Notice that the interest rate is significantly higher than the HELOC and home equity line of credit. This is because LOC is an unsecured line because it is not backed by your home. Although not having a mortgage or owning a home is going to cost you, you'll still win in the long run with this line if you use the money for an asset and not another liability.

Credit cards are often used incorrectly by the masses of people. The majority use credit cards to accumulate bad debt. The proper use should be to establish a huge credit line that can be accessed towards building wealth. It should be used as a tool for prosperity and not hardship. Change a simple habit of paying for your daily needs such as food, gas, and other essential supplies with cash or debit card and do it with a credit card instead.

Pay the amount spent on the credit card upon getting home and never pay interest on the card.

In fact, you can pay it weekly or even monthly but be sure to pay the entire balance by the due date to avoid interest.

You can do this very easily since you already have the money in cash or debit. Also, you'll enjoy good credit over time and credit limit increase. There are even perks that goes along with using your credit cards such as points and cash back rewards. The idea is to use a credit card as a tool that rewards you in all the ways I've mentioned, without being punished through high-interest rates payments as a result of misuse.

Be very responsible with credit cards, and you'll have a substantial credit limit and a low debt to credit ratio. In this case, you can use it occasionally to purchase assets when an opportunity presents itself, and you have no time to access money. After all, the asset you are buying will make you money that can be used to pay off the charge quickly.

You can also use it for the meantime while waiting for other forms of lending if you haven't already established any of the line of credit we've covered.

I'm concerned that folks that don't thoroughly understand this process may misuse it, so let me explain further. After all, I see this mistake all the time.

 One must be careful with this method because credit cards have a high-interest rate. They are currently around 16% -24% APR or annual percentage rate, meaning over 12 months. For example, a 24% APR cost 2% per month on all balances. Therefore a $100,000 balance will equate to paying $2000 in interest. If you run across an asset that can produce more, go for it. If the asset is still quite profitable but does not exceed the monthly minimum payment plus interest, then refrain from utilizing a credit card. The point is to pay off the charge as quickly as possible. Minimum monthly payments will not accomplish this goal.

Vendor line of credit is an excellent tool to utilize in establishing a business line of credit. New businesses need not worry because vendor line of credit is typically granted to non-established businesses regardless of how new it is. It usually comes in the form of 30-day net terms, meaning you'll have to pay in full by the end of the 30-day period. Before using this strategy, be sure to obtain a DUNS number from D&N or Duns and Bradstreet.

Proceed to establish vendor accounts with companies that supply items you use or sell and opt-in for their invoice me later option.

Pay the invoice on time as these vendors will report payments terms and history to the business credit reporting agencies. Use several companies for your supplies, and as they all report your history, your business credit begins to grow. Soon, you'll be able to apply for regular business credit as you would have established one in just a few short months. In fact, you will begin to get offers in the mail in no time.

There are many forms of retirement savings worldwide. In America, the most popular one is the 401K. It is a plan that makes provisions for eligible workers to invest in their own retirement. The employer is given incentives to sponsor the program on a tax-deferred basis by the internal revenue service. As a result, many established and profitable businesses participate. These companies match up to a specified amount of your contributions and invest it with a registered investment firm. Historically, 401K investments have done well. The benefit of a larger monthly dollar amount of investment is quite attractive, and so many employees do subscribe. The pre-tax money deducted from wage or salary is then invested in the stock market. As time goes on, gains are accumulated. The 401K account enables both employers and employees to benefit in tax deductions.

Savings from 401K can be utilized by borrowing from your own account and repaying with interest. It must be noted that borrowing from 401K should be done only if other forms of loans with lower interest is not available. Use the money to buy assets and not liabilities. Financially astute people use all loans to purchase assets only. The first contribution is pre-tax, but repayment of the money you lend is done using after-tax money; therefore, double taxation occurs at retirement. Always pay the loan back as quickly as possible. Remember that any loan balance has to be paid in its entirety within 60 days, in the event that your employment ends for whatever reason. The penalty of not paying if employment ends are income tax and an additional penalty of 10% for all persons under the age of fifty-nine years.

Another very popular one is called an IRA or Individual Retirement Account. It is similar to the previously mentioned retirement savings except there is no opportunity for company contribution.

The yearly contribution limit is $5,500 and $6,500 if you are fifty years old or older.

Although you are not allowed to borrow and repay, you can withdraw without penalty. The reason being that IRA is an after-tax contribution. Both the 401K and IRA are often used because there is no lender involved; therefore, no credit check is performed.

Again, if you take money from your retirement and use it for anything other than assets, which will produce higher returns, you are doing yourself a disservice.

Creativity

With the right mindset, you can utilize your creativity by seeking investors to join you in your quest for acquiring assets. In real estate, one such method is called syndication, but this strategy can be applied to acquiring any assets. It is a process where you bring in other investors to secure the capital needed for acquiring a property. If you evaluate an asset that will produce good profits, you can, in turn, afford to offer above normal competitive rate of return to such investors. I'll illustrate an example of creativity through a childish business I once had as an adolescent. This example can be applied to any business of any size.

At the age of nine, I had two small businesses. I managed to utilize an infinite rate of return at that age without having heard the phrase. The first was selling bread and the second, selling kerosene. Since this was a long time ago, the exact prices or details are not relevant. Here's the scenario: Let's say the kerosene cost $12 for a five-gallon bucket and it produces fifty 12-ounce bottles. Each bottle sells for $1, and I'm able to sell all fifty bottles per day.

First-day profit would be $20. I purchased the supplies needed such as all the fifty-second hand 12-ounce bottles for $18 and already had the five-gallon bucket. As a side note, all the bottles, as well as the five-gallon buckets, are reusable. The customers have their own empty bottles to swap when a sale is made. If I work every day for a year, the total revenue would be $7,300.

For a nine-year-old with no money, I can borrow the $30 needed to start the kerosene business from my investors. It can be my parents, friends, neighbors, or any other investor as long as they are guaranteed a profit.

Pursuit of ~~Happiness~~ Assets

I can literally pay back what I borrowed plus one 100% interest all by the end of the second day and still make a profit of $16. I would have made a whopping $2,920 in profits in 1 year. Not bad for any age when you start at zero. Since no market pays at 100% interest, my offer would be extremely attractive to any investor. I mean, as an investor, I would jump at an opportunity to invest at 100% interest in two days every chance I get.

If you want more profit for this kerosene business, simply duplicate the process.

Bring in some of your friends and pay them commissions to work for you in different neighborhoods.

As far as bringing in people, just imagine if you recruited 10 of your friends to do the same thing at a 50% commission or split and you supplied everything. All of a certain, a nine-year-old boy just made an annual profit of $14,510 from being creative and resourceful. Your friends are also happy because they started with nothing and now they're earning about $4 a day or $1,451 a year as adolescents.

If you study the concept illustrated above and truly understand it, you can apply it to any asset you wish to buy and generate the funds from zero. All you need for this method is specialized knowledge of the asset you wish to acquire and its returns. This way, you determine how much interest to pay investors and still remain profitable. With a good reputation, if you are able to do your due diligence properly and can see the potential, you can guarantee a specific attractive rate of return to your trusted investors.

Investors have everything to gain, especially if they cannot expect your rate of return from anywhere else. This applies to all assets, all sizes, and at all cost. The takeaway is that even a person that has no capital can still pursue assets. Having the knowledge to do it is an asset that can, in turn, be leverage with investors for mutual benefits.

Saving money is my least favorite because it takes time. The length of time varies based on your capacity to earn and save.

A skilled and specialized professional such as a doctor or a lawyer, if determined, may be able to save faster than a non-skilled worker. That said, a non-skilled worker may have fewer bills and therefore if committed, can save the capital needed in due time.

Not doing anything at all should not be an option. Anyone with the will and persistent can find a way to save. Even if it takes deprivation of some material wishes and longer than desired time to save, you will be victorious in the end.

When it comes to saving money, many think it's all about the extra money you put away into your savings. Many other actions help to either accelerate the process or increase the savings significantly.

First, one must remember that spending less means saving more. Simply taking an inventory of your expenditure may uncover multiple areas where spending can be reduced or even eliminated.

You don't really need entertainment to survive, so cutting recurring cable and its related services in the name of savings should be considered. If you eat out multiple times a week, that too can be eliminated for some time since eating out can add up quickly. Instead, you can buy and cook your food, and you'll produce a noticeable difference in savings. If you have paid services such as landscaping, pest control, and housekeeping, etc., you can halt all those services until you've reached your savings necessary to start your asset acquisition.

Lastly, get rid of habitual small debts that takes away money from you monthly, such as department store credit cards, other credit cards, rent-to-own items, payday loans, and so on. This practice will free up money that can be saved.

Buying a certified pre-owned vehicle instead of a new vehicle will save you tremendous amounts of cash. New cars lose their values by 20% the first year and an additional 10% yearly so a 4-year old car can be purchased at half off. These are just a few smart adjustments to make if your goal is to save money. It may sound like deprivation; however, if all the other more pleasant ways of money generation is not an option for you, perhaps saving might be.

Leverage Your Ability

Knowing how to leverage your ability to build wealth is a great asset. Assemble a team of professionals that pertains to the type of wealth you are pursuing. Install systems to automate aspect of your wealth creation process wherever possible. Acquire assets that increase in equity over time and produces cash flow indefinitely. Start small and expand as to realize gains or profits. Evaluate to see areas that are working well or needs innovation.

Where to begin varies slightly from person to person. For instance, a person that has bad debt would begin with my FREE Debt Elimination e-Course that's accessible through Devise Wealth Mastermind Facebook Group. Membership is free as well. Simply answer three questions, and you're in. The support within this group is definitely an asset to all. Undertaking any project entails planning. The answer to the question of initial capital, credit, and leveraging should all be in place. Any real asset would require these things, and you should already have them or access as needed. Next agenda is to examine and choose what projects to be associated with carefully.

Money can be earned in several ways. It can be earned as income, passive, dividends, and royalties, etc. Your unique situation will determine the source of capital. For many, it's a job and maybe a part-time or temporary gig. Some may already have a business but haven't begun acquiring any real wealth, regardless of your current circumstance. The focus is to raise enough money to do the deal. Allocate some of your income into a short term savings specifically for undertaking the project. Simultaneously work on your credit and bring it to at least a score of 800. When you have achieved these two steps, you can now use leverage to secure lending.

Pursue projects that are system based. This means that it should be equipped with processes that makes up a system so that it can be run by virtually anyone who can read and follow the documentation — either fully automated or mostly performed by an automatic process. For the case of real estate, undertake turnkey properties. An example of a turnkey property is one that is identified, rehabbed if necessary and managed by a third party. Your job would be to do the deal. The third party's job is to make ready, rent the units, and deposit payments into your bank account. Do not contract with any company that does not guarantee occupancy or pays the rent after ninety days of a vacancy in any given year. The fee for these companies are usually 10% or less of the monthly rent. Choose companies that have the ability to project your cash flow from investment.

Due to the nature of turnkey real estate, it can be acquired anywhere in the United States and many places overseas. Remember, you are not after the property. Instead, you are going after the business of such property. Consequently, you are detached and free from any emotional connection. You are only concerned with the performance, not how it looks or where it's located. That said, choose a reputable company that cares about the tenants and follows all applicable laws concerning the housing industry. Make sure the company understand your personal policy of providing safe, clean, functioning housing, and very good customer service.

In the case of pursuing investment in the stock market, seek companies with a winning historical data and leadership of the

Pursuit of ~~Happiness~~ Assets

executives. Investments can be very hands-off as compared to business and real estate. You can simply buy stocks for the long term and expect an average of 8% annual growth or higher without doing anything. There are cases where 15% to 25% growth are typical. Imagine gaining twenty-five dollars on every hundred dollars invested or two hundred and fifty thousand for every million. The returns alone would enable you to acquire subsequent assets to make you wealthy.

A million dollars is not difficult to reach, especially with mutual funds. The Standard & Poor's (S&P) index for an example has an average gain of 10% over the last 60 years. Even with 2008 being the worst year in those 60 years when its stock fell by 37%, its average was almost 9%. So just investing two hundred dollars a month in mutual funds for fifty years will yield around three million dollars at 10% and that's being conservative. To put things in perspective, that's a 96% growth because you would have only invested one hundred twenty thousand over the 50 years' time. The key is to start early, as a matter of fact, start now. The Standard & Poor's typically performs lower than a small capitalization mutual fund type so it may yield an even higher yearly average over time.

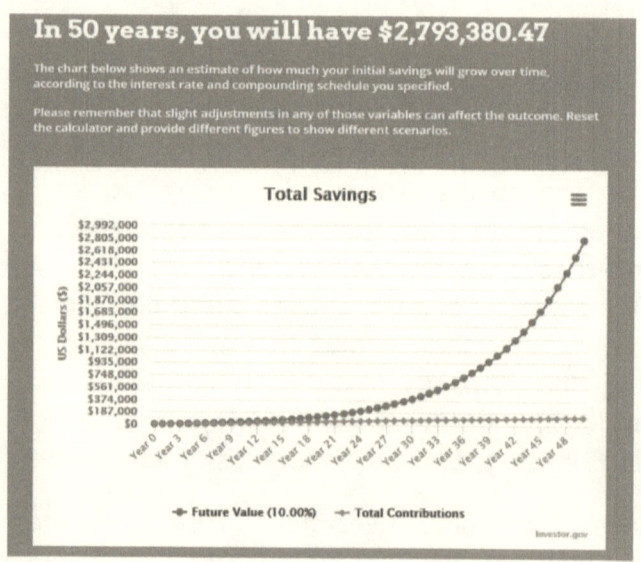

A person that aspires to build wealth without the demands of running a business or real estate can undertake a low-risk investment such as stocks or mutual funds. As always, when one learns before undertaking, he or she will have more insight and confidence to proceed. Particularly, doing this will ensure that you choose mutual funds that out-performs The Standard & Poor's and consequently, the stock market as a whole. The data is easily accessible as your broker can pull it up within minutes.

Even after learning, investing still benefits from the use of professionals. If you've watched some of my YouTube Videos, you know the analogy that I often use is not letting your doctor work on your car or mechanic operate on your body. These people are trained for their respective specialties. The same applies to stockbrokers. Yes, you'll have to pay either a loaded fee or a commission as well as a management fee. Even though non-loaded do exist, many believe it is embedded in the management fees. The key is to learn so that you'll know what the average management fee should be at the time of your investment.

Let's say you are a first-time real estate investor. My sentiment is start small, gain field experience, and then expand as large as you can leverage other people's resources. The premise is that you want to invest in a single-family rental real estate property. You have educated yourself about the ins-and-outs of it all, and have your team in place. A down payment is available, and your credit is great. Tenant prospect looks good as well. The deal is estimated to cash flow five hundred dollars a month. Virtually every aspect of due diligence has been completed, including a title search. There are no liens on the property. Inspection has also been done, and the lender has already sent someone to do the appraisal. Papers are ready to be signed. Ownership of the mortgage is imminent, and a tenant is standing by to move in.

As you can see, a real estate investor has more than one or two steps to complete. It's a series of things that must be checked before finishing the race. The last of which is getting your first rent payment from your tenant or a check from your buyer. Different projects dictate the level of understanding that's required. Not familiarizing yourself with the project is risky and should be avoided. Buying a property starts from raising capital and establishing great credit to using leverage and acquiring the asset. The process ends when said assets have begun to produce profits.

When you undertake an online business, you must answer the question of what products or services to sell, how to market it and price point, and how to structure support. Having a great support team will keep your customers happy. Online business is viable because it is typically less expensive to start and can be constructed fairly quickly with opportunities to scale. It can be operated from virtually anywhere on a part-time basis. In most cases, you won't need any inventory or equipment. Additional employees can be hired later, but you can start by yourself.

There are so many ways you can go on this one, yet the end result should be the same. It's about having a sales funnel that guides potential customers to quality product and services that you own. You can also be an affiliate of such products.

Typical earnings for affiliate products can range from 5% to 90% commission. Physical products pays a lesser commission, and digital pays higher. The key is offering things that are useful and important to your customers. One little niche can satisfy this criterion.

I know many people that have built substantial businesses by serving customers online with what they want and need. The one thing in common is that all of these entrepreneurs use a variety of methods to provide value to their customers. Included in their methods are digital marketing such as short message service or SMS, email, and social media.

It's all about your style of thinking and attitude.

"Both poverty and riches are the offspring of thought." - *Napoleon Hill*

CHAPTER THREE:

True Independence

Another driving force for asset pursuit is the attainment of true independence. This chapter aims at defining true independence and what it may look like. It is not a one size fits all as this subject is relative to values, cultures, religion, and a host of other important areas of human activity. Collectively, however, you'll have a glimpse of true independence for most people. What might be done to not only pursue but attain it, and the benefits are all covered here.

A system that enables conversion of assets into cash flow continually, facilitates true independence more than any other thing. As a result, one is able to make decisions without fear of losing this status and becoming dependent.

There are many such systems created year after year for the last few centuries. In modern times, new powered machines and factories were created that enabled mass production, therefore flourishing the industrial revolution. It continued with electrical and telephone technology, which in turn made way for production lines. Prior to that, things were done manually and at a much slower pace.

Today, look at all humankind is able to do, with the inception of the internet, smartphone, cloud computing, and other technologies of that nature.

All these developments are assets and much more are yet to be developed. Besides making things easier, these assets have spawned many businesses that produce massive cash flow. Just look at how we access data, consume media, how we shop, and travel. When something is created to simplify our lives, the creator reaps the benefits in a major way.

This simplification also allows the creation of emerging assets in a uniformed way each time, and consequently more efficient. The results are considerable wealth. Aside from building considerable wealth, systems should be turnkey to a large degree, such that it can operate with or without the owner's physical presence. It takes time to documents processes and procedures in an easy to understand and execute fashion.

Once it is completed, however, it can be duplicated over and over again. The cost of positioning yourself for true independence by automating systems is minimal compared to the benefits. Whatever is important to you can be attained. More free time lends itself to better health and knowledge. Your network of connections grows, and you feel more secured, but the most important is the capability of helping others.

Wealth

Many see wealth as a way of achieving true independence. On the contrary, enormous wealth without a means to generate cash flow will be exhausted in a matter of time. That's because it's not being replenished. It's like taking candy out of the jar continuously without refilling.

How fast wealth is lost depends on your nature and rate of spending. Regardless of the wealth resource, it must have the ability to produce income on an ongoing basis for anyone to experience true independence.

In addition, cash from wealth should be backed by a more stable asset such as business, real estate and stock investment. Businesses can be risky if not properly evaluated and understood. When implementing a wealth plan through business, one has to know their strengths and weaknesses and enlist qualified people to fill the areas of deficiencies.

For instance, a medical facility owned by a specialist doctor needs an experienced human resource manager, a lawyer, and an accountant that specializes in healthcare related services, a robust practice management system, merchant services, malpractice insurance and a marketer. It wouldn't be practical for the specialist doctor to operate successfully without these set of people.

The previous paragraph illustrated an example of building wealth through a service-based business like a medical facility and what is needed to ensure a smooth operation. Let's take a look at building wealth through products-based business like DME or durable medical equipment. Slight variations apply to other product-based businesses in retail. Buying an existing profitable DME business is an option that will immediately produce cash flow upon purchase. This method requires being able to properly evaluate the business to make sure you don't overpay. Like anything else in business, consulting is just a phone call away if you don't have the expertise. There are many factors to examine, so an inexperienced buyer should definitely use professional help in the acquisition.

If building this same business from the ground up is more feasible, it can be done without any major hurdle. First, you must secure a building. My first choice is always to buy as opposed to lease.

This method ensures equity for yourself in a few years, a benefit that leasing never produces in a million years. Since we're focused on building wealth, allowing room for add-ons in the future, or building more than needed and renting the remainder should not be overlooked. Permits and setup will follow, then inspections will be next.

Proceed to establish line of credits with various vendors that will supply the DME. These vendor accounts will usually have a net 30 to a net 60 requirement. This simply means all invoices must be paid per 30 or 60 days. Upon completion of permits and the other listed items, an inspector will visit to verify the business. They will also review pertinent documentation. If everything checks out, you will be granted a license to operate. While waiting to be licensed, roll out your advertisement, and adequately staff the operation.

You can register with in-network health insurance companies as well as Medicare and Medicaid if you're in the United States. These in-network insurances will account for over 50% of your revenue. The remainder will be walk-ins and private pay customers. The healthcare service and product-based businesses I covered are just two examples of how to build wealth through businesses. Either one, if done correctly, will catapult you into the path of true independence. Of course, neither will make you rich overnight; however, great profits over time is your que to duplicate the results with a second establishment and beyond.

There are thousands of other assets in the form of a business, and one should tailor their choice around skill, interest, experience, and passion. In other words, pursue assets that you understand the most. That said, real estate, as well as stocks and bonds, should be pursued, in addition, for a business to enjoy the maximum benefits of building wealth.

Taking the time to learn or using consulting should be at the top of your agenda. Building wealth takes a little more effort, but the rewards and legacy are incomparable. Much more about building wealth with business, real estate, and investment in the stock market will be covered in section III; Asset Power Moves: What and How?

Health

Working enormous hours indefinitely to make ends meet is not good for your health. It is a true statement whether you have a plan for wealth building or just working to pay liabilities. The pattern of such exercise is not sustainable if having good health is important to you. In the course of one full day, sleep and rest should take half while work and recreation takes the other half. When the body and the mind lack sufficient rest and relaxation for an extended period of time, the results could be a weakened immune system as well as chronic illnesses.

You don't have true independence if you are working around the clock for whatever reason. In a case of being an employee, one should at least position themselves to have the ability to secure a job that compensates enough with just one eight-hour shift.

Having a second job or working overtime consistently will eventually manifest itself in the form of declining health. For these reasons, either downsize your lifestyle in exchange for adequate sleep, rest and recreation or complete the necessary skills for a higher paying job. Components of achieving true independence should be built into your plan.

The same holds true in terms of working hours that exceed the previous threshold mentioned even for wealth builders.

Pursuit of ~~Happiness~~ Assets

The plan is to put systems in place that will enable automation wherever possible and one that can thrive with or without your physical presence.

Automating your source for cash flow means more time for other things of interest, especially plenty of sleep. Several stages of a plan to true independence takes hard work, dedication, and excessive hours, but it's only temporary, and the payoff is worth it.

Even when working hard towards a goal of acquiring assets that will afford you the lifestyle of which you dream, your plan should be well organized and structured. It should include a reasonable amount of work per day and built-in breaks to avoid exhaustion.

Nothing is so important, not even building wealth, to the extent that anyone should risk their long-term health. An efficient and well-executed plan gets the job done in less time. Stay relentless in your pursuit, and soon you'll realize true independence.

Another benefit of true independence is health because you can afford to give your body and mind all the rest it needs. Your asset is generating cash flow even when you're asleep. Better yet, you can afford the finest in health and fitness. How you pamper or take care of yourself should not be compromised. Having adequate relaxation, high-grade nutrition, and healthcare is sure to produce great health. More free time, in essence, accentuates better health.

Essentially, what the school system has failed to teach is the adequate education of wealth building. The kind that should deeply familiarize students with assets, and not treat it like it's outside the scope of their indoctrination. It seems people have to venture out to get this important education. As a consequence, students graduate with a sense of getting a job to pay for all the material things that continuously flashes in their face through the television and at the shopping centers.

What is needed is specialized knowledge of monetizing your interest, skill, gift, and talent. I call it specialize knowledge because everyone is not trained on how to utilize it effectively.

This gives the recipient an advantage over others and generates recurring income when appropriately monetized. Innovation is compulsory as time progress. Make it a policy to remain in the forefront or others will attempt not only to advance pass your level but possibly put you out of business. Simply pay attention and stay ahead of the trends. Having specialized knowledge and applying it to build wealth converts into a favorable outcome. This act can forge more free time, which in turn permits the facilitation of better health.

Connection and Security

As an entrepreneur, it is important to have specific links to people that will help with your vision for mutual benefits. In fact, the level of difficulty will increase without the right connections at various intervals of your network. When you have connections in place, you can reach out and get things done. A successful real estate investor has connections to a realtor/broker, loan officer, property manager, and others. These connections will enable the investor to proceed with business smoothly without major setbacks. Locating a property all the way to collecting rent from tenants can be seamless as a result of the proper connection. In the end, you'll have the security of true independence for formulating connections with competent people in their respective areas.

Whether it's specialized knowledge or connection, the relationship is mutually beneficial to all parties. All parties stand to benefit from any deal that is successfully closed. Among the benefits are compensation and especially resources made available in a quick, seamless fashion.

As time goes on, the size of your network of connections will grow to allow more options and avenue to get things done. The feeling of true independence is vague without the right connections. Connect yourself with people that have the best experience in the asset of your interest. Learn from them but make your own decisions. Remember, true independence is the ability to consider trusted experts' recommendation and the freedom to choose another option.

The sense of security one feels when truly independent is very significant. When others are faced with company downsizing or shutdown, a person with passive income systems in place is not affected. That is the kind of security true independence produces. Often, employers downsize when needed without regards to its employee's welfare. Right or wrong, it is up to each person to secure his or her own future. Those that heed doesn't find themselves at the short end of the stick when this occurs. Avoid losing your job one day by working towards true independence even if you're currently an employee. Create your own stability.

It's about planning out a future of assets that produces cash flow. It takes ambition and persistent but not doing it should not be an option. Even in the best-case scenario where an employee works until retirement, the money does not last. Even without any layoff, the contributed money into a savings plan diminishes quickly. The rising cost of healthcare alone will deplete the retirement funds at an alarming rate. At this point, most people are forced to go back to work if they're able. Most of the time, the post-retirement job pays much less, and conditions become stressful. I believe it is better to acquire assets that will produce income continually for the enjoyment of a real sense of security.

Controlling Your Destiny

You can control the type of assets you acquire by assessing yourself, your spending behavior, and your understanding of such assets. Business takes lots of resources such as time, talent, money, systems, leadership, and management, etc. You are responsible for assembling it all. If planned correctly, it should become turnkey once it is propelled into motion. Let's say for an example that a young couple wanted to venture into the healthcare industry offline and open a medical supply business. They have educated themselves about the subject. All the outcome of your research suggests that it would be a profitable business with an attractive ROI. The decision to go forward has been made. The process of undertaking any offline business can be overwhelming if not approached in an organized and systematic fashion. It begins with you finding a place. Buying your own building will have a similar procedure as buying a home for the most part. Leasing, however, is different. Staying vigilant throughout and reading the lease documents thoroughly is very important.

The couples' decision to start a business in the healthcare industry selling medical supplies is weighed against similar offline businesses. They're in control when the results of the research indicate that this type of business is lucrative. The numbers all make sense and discussions of whether to buy a building or rent one is now taking place. If the couple prepared themselves well, they can purchase their own building.

When you lease, you are essentially paying the mortgage for your landlord. Although there are circumstances that warrants leasing, this is not the case for this project. Moving forward by securing a mortgage, means this couple will realize an equity growth with time, as land and building historically appreciates. One day if and when they decide to sell the business, they can either collect monthly rent from the buyer or sell the business at a significantly higher price that includes the building. If this couple thoroughly understands my system of paying off any mortgage in five years, their building would be paid in full. The value should have increased dramatically or possibly doubled. Any similar scenario where there is no control, it would have been a less favorable result.

Now that we are clear about the building, let's dive into how to assemble the business. The couple would set up the place, fill out the required applications for permits and licenses. Upon completion of the inspections, the officials would grant them the necessary documents to open. During the setup process, marketing would be in full effect as well as employee orientation and training. All contract with vendors and suppliers would have also been completed during this phase. In fact, the store would be totally equipped for the grand opening.

There are many types of real estate that can be controlled for profit. It requires many of the same resources but can be semi-hands off. You can contract a large portion of it to professionals such as realtors, brokers, property managers, accountants, and lawyers. This is an area where you can raise money fairly quickly with what is known as wholesaling. In a nutshell, wholesaling is finding properties well below market value and selling it to another investor for profit. The process can be time-consuming, so partnering with a company that has systems already in place will cut the time in half.

Many of task involves finding motivated, absentee, or distress sellers and putting the property under contract, then buying it yourself or selling it to another investor. You have the ability to sell the contract to another investor because you have an equitable interest in the property. For starters, your local courthouse can supply you with a list of probate houses. Title and lien checks are a must when wholesaling, so no surprises arise down the line.

Before attempting to control a property, you must know the after-repair value by aggregating the sales comparable in that area. You must also know the cost of rehabilitating the property. Simply subtract 65% from the after-repair value plus rehab cost to arrive at what your profit should be. Wholesaling is a viable option because no cash is needed initially. Besides, you can make a handsome profit without actually buying the property.

An example would be finding a seller and making an offer that's less than the after-repair value minus let's say 20% rehab and 65% investor price. As a wholesaler, you will make a 15% profit. If you buy the property yourself, you'll make more.

Investment in the stock market can be completely turnkey because you can virtually have a professional broker design a strategy for you to buy shares of stocks and mutual funds etc. You will not have to manage anyone or assemble any team for overseeing your investments. Your money should grow at an annual average of 10% or higher per year. Be sure to diversify to minimize risk.

Investment requires the least amount of your time if you use a broker and invest in growth mutual funds. I tend to like it because historically, it outperforms the S&P 500, which is a good representation of the stock market as a whole. There are so many companies you can invest in, and with the help of a good broker or investment advisor, you stand to acquire wealth without much effort.

Ask your broker for data on the best-performing stocks. Look at the data and have him or her explain things you don't understand. When you are clear on the company and its data, proceed to buy shares. It is truly a game of time. The longer you invest, the richer you become. Investing what you'd pay as a car payment for 50 years will make you 6 million or more. That is simply fascinating to invest $400 a month and get that kind of return. The fact that you don't have to operate a business or real estate is the icing on the cake.

The principle of always buying assets and never liabilities is important, and so is buying an asset that requires little or no work. Just make sure there's a positive cash flow. Once you begin to acquire assets, there must be a system in place to control them. That system too must be turnkey. In other words, a management system to manage the managers. This system should have all the proper organization and protocols of engaging the overall leaders of the various companies. In a way, this system would replicate an enterprise.

There should be methods and procedures that can be understood and administered by anyone. At this level, decisions are made on buying other profitable assets and selling under-performing assets. Advance strategies are implemented here to minimize tax and other liabilities while maximizing income. Your team should have a cohesiveness and understanding with regards to your vision and must act in the best interest of such vision.

Help Others

There is no gratifying feeling better than the ability to help others that are in need. If you share this sentiment, you'll be glad to know that being truly independent makes it possible. Being in this position allows the giver to give in whatever capacity they desire. Aside from employing qualified people, you can also help with charity. So many charitable causes may hit close to home for folks that build their wealth from the bottom up. They tend to recognize people that stand where they once stood. It becomes second nature to lend a helping hand.

My personal experience extends pass, helping my clients. Many people have reached out to me for consultation in matters of business, real estate, credit repair, and building wealth in general. I always help. However, I can.

Not everyone that I've helped purchased my courses, books, or other products. I figured, my duty is to provide value for free because it will lead people to my products at a later time. So far to my knowledge, that has been the case for many, as people sometimes message after purchasing one of my products.

Even just the free publications like my articles or my how-to videos are helpful to many. It is evidenced by all the thank you I frequently get. Educating the masses to get their finances in order and build wealth is a calling, I gladly answered well over a decade ago. The results have been amazing.

Positioning myself with assets has afforded me the time to be of service to others. Whether it's a Facebook post, email, or telephone consultation, I take pride in helping others. If an extensive knowledge is needed, I then direct people to one of my products that will best suit them. My open access policy ensures that all who want my help gets it. If I can play a role in making you truly independent, I'm all in.

When you have given to a multitude of charities with causes that's near and dear to your heart, perhaps starting your own non-profit to tend to such causes is a great initiative to do more. Although there are less fortunate people all over the globe. My experience points me back to Africa, where imperialism, colonialism, and neocolonialism have deprived children of the basic necessities of life. To date, there are millions that do not have access to clean water, sanitation, nutritious food, shelter, and education. These are all potential areas with great opportunities to be of service.

The rewards of taking an interest in any charity is the feeling of accomplishment. One feels great when they've made a difference in the life of the less fortunate. This type of project also teaches you about humanity beyond the limits of your country and allows you to see the world differently and with compassion.

A debt of gratitude and appreciation for the cultures and values of others sets in. Overall, a person that help others reaps the rewards of an abundant life. The more you give, the more you receive.

"True independence is the ability to consider trusted experts recommendation and the freedom to choose another option." - Kenneth Botwe

SECTION II

Asset Power Moves: When and How?

There isn't a wrong time to pursue assets. In fact, it serves you and your family better to begin immediately without hesitation. The greatest enemy of accomplishment is procrastination. It can linger on until your time is up. Beginning the pursuit now means that you have disabled the enemy and therefore the possibilities are endless. Ask yourself why not now and eliminate every excuse that comes to mind. Remember that nothing happens without action.

Start performing the actions stipulated by your roadmap we discus in section one. It can be smaller steps initially and bigger ones as you progress. The important thing is taking the steps. Consult with experts and experience people along the way to avoid common mistakes and to stay on the right projector of success.

In this section, you're going to uncover the answers to the questions when and how to pursue assets. You'll learn that the time is now in terms of at least laying the groundwork for pursuing assets.

Pursuit of ~~Happiness~~ Assets

Because assets pursuit is a long-term ambition, you'll explore the how to ensure your legacy continuity with your family and estate as a whole. The process of planning, protection mechanism and teaching your children to do the same will all be examined. It is my hope that this section motivates you to take action now.

CHAPTER FOUR:

Pursue Assets now

The right time to pursue assets is now. To move closer to achieving true independence, a miracle must occur, or you must take action. The odds of a miracle is much greater than taking matters into your own hands. As hard as your circumstance may seem, you will realize that taking action was much easier than it seemed. Devise a plan, implement it, make periodic evaluations and adjustments. This is the premise of this chapter. It's a simple, easy to understand method to achieving success with assets through careful planning.

Mindset

If you're not able to effectively manage your resources for building wealth, you simply need a mindset shift and seek more financial education. There's absolutely nothing wrong with not knowing as long as you're mindful that you don't know. When one is aware, that person can begin to take steps to change their circumstances. You have to believe because not believing that you can create wealth is an enemy within. Every nonbeliever has their own unique reason, but I can assure you that anyone can build wealth with assets.

It starts with believing. Believe it in your core, your soul, and with all your heart. Not believing get you nowhere; however, there's a level of commitment that transcends into actions when one accepts or feel sure about something. The feeling that you can build wealth is one that only you can invite. Be realistic and conduct some soul searching, and if you conclude that you don't have what it takes, ask yourself why. Challenging yourself will sometimes unmask the truth which can enable you to make whatever adjustments that's needed. Re-examine again after some time to see if you're now a believer. Often after this exercise, there's a change of heart.

If you've never pursued assets before, you must learn. Before a child could walk and talk, that child had to learn. Granted, the child may have fallen a few times, but that did not deter the child from trying. They learned, and now getting around is a breeze. Learn how to acquire assets and building wealth will be as easy as walking. Study someone wealthy by following their work and reaching out to them for mentorship when feasible. Feel free to get all the free publications and if it's truly helping you, do not hesitate to purchase their products for sale. It's a win-win because you get the insight needed and support your mentor at the same time. That said when you have thoughtfully applied the systems I've outlined here and need additional assistance, feel free to reach out to me.

One of the most natural things a person can do is apply the lessons they've learned, so it's therefore unusual not to do so. Begin your quest to building wealth. Start small and set goal to grow at various milestones. Continue to increase your efforts and watch your wealth expand like a balloon. I assure you, it's a beautiful thing, but you've got to start the process. When you compare the daunting task of going to work for someone for 40 years versus having your own system of wealth building that can free you from any employer, the decision should be quite straightforward.

Devise a Wealth Plan

Nothing happens until you devise an asset pursuit plan, so begin now without hesitation. It all starts with a thought. Document your thinking and then re-organize it into a plan. Do you have any unique talent, skill, experience, or training?

If the area of most familiarity in terms of asset is where your interest lies, you are already on the right path. The first set of questions that must be answered are what problems and opportunities have I identified?

The answer should be beneficial to a community large enough to support your asset. If it's not, return to the drawing board and identify another set of problems and opportunities.

The idea is to get the type of assets that solves a problem and produces cash flow regularly. It's about sustainable cash flow. Pursue an asset that generates money and then re-invested it for more. Aside from what you need, remaining proceeds should always be put back into the asset or another asset.

The proceeds should never be allowed to remain idle because money loses its value over time when it doesn't move. This phenomenon is due to general price increases and a decrease in the buying power of money.

That's right; inflation affects money that is not put to work so pursue assets now. The important thing is to begin by formulating a plan.

It does not need to be a perfect plan. Periodic reviews will reveal areas of improvements and adjustments can be made at that time.

Pursuit of ~~Happiness~~ Assets

A person who wished to invest in the stock market, for example, would conduct research specifically on it. He or she would get familiar with the securities of their interest. Regardless of the asset, the next step after the problem-opportunity research phase is to analyze what is required to solve the problem.

The level of research, however, depends on the magnitude of the investment. Investing one percent of your cash would not require an extensive effort of learning as it would ten percent.

You may start with a small investment after basic understanding and gradually add more as you gain a better understanding. This strategy allows implementation without the delay of seeking expert knowledge. Of course, consulting with an expert is advisable as it reduces the learning curve. Scale up as you become more knowledgeable and confident.

How you understand important factors in stock trading such as management, historical performance, trends, forecast, competition, and innovation, it gets easier with time as you begin to study these essentials.

It could be as early as months or as late as years, but your understanding is sure to evolve. By all means, modifications in strategies and processes would occur.

This example holds true for people who want to pursue other forms of assets, especially if starting small and scaling up is part of the plan. Beware, it would not work quite as well for major undertakings because the room for error is much narrower.

Apart from the fundamentals, experience is the best teacher, so proceeding with a plan that has room for growth is essential for the overall health of the pursuit. As stated, always seek some assistance from experienced and competent people when devising a wealth plan. There are so many bells and whistles that can be missed or overlook by ambitious but inexperienced candidates. In consulting with experts, many mistakes are eliminated, and a smoother operation is attained. The help you receive can come from anywhere as long as it's credible and has substantial success record. Generally, you want assistance from people and institutions that have already accomplished what you wish to accomplish. Even paid consulting is necessary in most cases, especially if doing so will save you time, money, and maybe even frustration.

In essence, pursuing assets should be a well thought out and calculated idea. It should be incorporated into a plan with help from industry experts. As a CEO of your asset pursuit, be familiar with every aspect without neglecting necessary consulting. Although not all ventures may require outside help, those that can be substantiated should be done whenever feasible. At least, it would place you in a comfortable situation, thus allowing you to grow more rapidly. So whether it's business, stock market, real estate, or other form of assets, starting now can never be over-emphasized. Once the plan is complete, the next step would be implementation.

Implement your plan

The process of implementation is not easier, even if you've got a well thought out plan. This stage requires careful planning as well with assigned responsibilities to team members, and a clear path for communication among the members. A clear vision must be properly understood by all involved, and a system of accountability should already be in place. When you are ready to implement a plan, it is advisable to test it for some time before rolling it out to the general public. In many cases, this testing stage enables you to see and correct potential issues that may arise.

Just like technology rollouts where alpha and beta testing is essential, all products and services should also be tested by a selected group to capture problems and ensure quality. In the end, you want the customer experience to be great. Your business cannot thrive if you don't get this right. Keep in mind that every major thing you do in pursuit of assets needs to be organized in a series of easy to follow plan and implementation.

When you test your plan before implementation, you'll also gain deeper awareness of your product or service; therefore, you can produce a top-quality customer experience. As I proclaimed that planning should be done tactically with the help of a seasoned professional, so should the implementation. Be sure to define your key performance indicators or KPI, which is asset specific. Your brand and reputation are an asset, and care should be taken not to turn it into a liability.

This can happen if planning and implementation is executed poorly. For these reasons, careful evaluations should be conducted during the testing stages. Even the selected group for testing should represent real targeted customers.

Consequently, properly devised and executed plan should produce a product or service that brings profits indefinitely. Track your progress regularly during the implementation stages.

Evaluations allow you to answer some important questions about your products and services. Just as the research revealed customer needs, evaluating the customer experience will equip you with a firsthand account of whether your product or service is a hit or miss.

More importantly, you'll know areas of sustainability or improvements. Since all of this occurs before putting out your product or service, all the customer sees at the end is your superior product or service.

Evaluate and Make Adjustments

Nearly every plan requires modification at some point in time. Gaining insight, unforeseen developments, re-targeting, and program improvement are just a few examples of why it is intelligent to evaluate your asset plan. To maximize the profit potential, the owner of an asset should be the expert of that particular asset. It isn't up to someone to motivate an owner of an asset. He or she should always stay on top of evaluations and be decisive in making necessary adjustments.

Gaining insight is a matter of evaluating and uncovering what happened and whether to do more, less, or stop it altogether. Other indicators will also reveal why it happened, which is very important in making the adjustments.

Review the collected data to see where adjustments may be needed. Having insight into these two factors are sure to assist in determining actions that should be taken.

There are unforeseen developments that evaluating can reveal.

The adjustment could be a matter of re-targeting, but not having the ability to see, will prevent you from doing so. Blockbuster videos would probably still exist had they evaluated, seen, and re-targeted their customers online through digital subscription or viewing. This is just one example of how detrimental not evaluating your asset could be.

Even if it's not detrimental to your type of asset, evaluating will still afford you the assessment needed to improve. Improving, in most cases, means an increase to the bottom line. I don't know of any asset that couldn't benefit from improvements. The type and to what extent can be revealed through asset plan evaluation.

"The man who moves a mountain begins by carrying away small stones." – Confucius

CHAPTER FIVE:

Long Live Assets after Your Death

Think long term when you think assets. After all, it's not like a valueless item or a fast depreciating possession. A real asset that has appreciating value and produces cash flow should be preserved for legacy. These assets should not dissipate after the owner's demise. Asset protection precautions should be taken to ensure that your assets survive and outlives you. There are many types and levels of ensuring your assets are protected.

At a minimum, protect your assets by separating it from yourself. You can achieve legal separation of your assets by forming an entity for it, such as a limited liability company or a corporation.

As long as you leave your assets in your name or a sole proprietorship, it goes when you go. In other words, it dissolves when you die. Correctly structuring it however means it outlives you. The next thing is to ensure you protect your assets from natural, human-made disaster, theft, and liability. We'll explore this topic further and in greater detail throughout this chapter.

Asset Protection

All wealth must be adequately protected no matter the means used to acquire it. Proper structure such as incorporating and insurances where needed are a must. All efforts should be made to separate yourself from your wealth. Asset protection means separating your various means of generating wealth, so one has nothing to do with another. It entails protecting your assets at all times. Place your assets in a safe, legal structure. This action will ensure that your assets are protected from all types of bad actors. If you have not read my Asset Protection Mindset article which reiterates why it is so essential to separate yourself from your wealth by incorporating, please do so. It demonstrates how a simple precaution can safeguard your assets from considerably huge risks.

Any substantial asset should be treated like a business. Whether it's a business itself, real estate, or investment, take the time to structure it properly. As I mentioned, to protect your assets, you must have a clear legal distinction between you and your assets. For instance, you own a house and have decided to buy and flip houses. Your first action should be to incorporate your business. By doing so, the business stands on its own. If any issues arise outside of the real estate business, no one can successfully go after your house in a lawsuit. Without the articles of formation in an LLC or incorporation, a plaintiff can win judgment order on anything that you own.

Asset protection serves many more purposes. Besides the legal separation between you and your assets, purchasing insurance is a form of asset protection. When you have adequate insurance, any loss or damage would be covered, therefore preserving your assets. Insuring your assets works the same way as your auto and home. When the unforeseen occurs, the insurance company will pay, and your asset will remain in-tact. There's no logical reason to not insure valuable assets.

Same things apply to intellectual properties such as trademark, systems, and things of that nature. These assets can be plagiarized or stolen, but having asset protection means your attorney can take legal action to correct violators. There are no shortage of violators, so protecting your assets serves as a deterrent, and they ultimately go when there are no protections in place.

As you can see, the need for a sound mindset in asset protection is very important when you have things of value. Simple precaution and a little investment for safeguarding your assets will save you from unnecessary loss in the litigious society of today. If you take extreme care in protecting your assets, it will serve as a deterrent and plaintiff's potential lawyers will refuse to accept the case on contingency fees. The would-be plaintiff, most likely wouldn't want to pay lawyer fees upfront, so they'll be more likely open to remedies other than a lawsuit.

Asset protection is necessary for every business in every industry as long as there's value. I can recall an incident that caused the demise of a thriving auto repair shop in North Carolina a little over a decade ago. A customer brought her vehicle in for repair. A few days later she picked up the car and got into an accident. It was alleged that the steering wheel came off while driving. The case went to court, and the shop owners were found to be negligent. The ruling was that the mechanic did not follow the method and procedure for repairing the car and therefore was at fault. Consequently, the shop owner's lost the lawsuit, and the plaintiff was awarded a large sum of cash.

The owners could not raise the money to settle the lawsuit. As a result, they were forced to sell the shop to settle. It was either sell the shop or risk losing their houses and other assets. This entire incident was a tragedy that could have been avoided. First, there should have been a protocol in place for a supervisor or a master mechanic to do a final inspection of all repairs before releasing vehicles to their owners. Second, the owners should have taken the right structure when they formulated the business. A two-member LLC would have sufficed, or an S-corporation also known as an S-corp. Either of these legal structure would have immediately separated the owners and their shop from all other assets. Third, a general liability or GL insurance in the amount of at least 1 million should have been taken on day one of the shop's operation.

There are additional asset protection that would have prevented the total loss of the shop; however, just the ones I mentioned above would have been sufficient. If they had just the ones I listed, the entire incident would have been prevented. The vehicle would have been repaired correctly, and therefore, the question of lawsuit would be non-existent. In the event that a lawsuit do arise, it would have been limited to the shop only, and not the owners and their personal assets. The shop then would inform the GL insurance company, and they would activate their lawyers to handle the case. If their lawyers feel they could not win the case, they would then settle for no more than the insurance coverage of 1 million dollars. The owners would keep their shop, as well as all their personal assets. There would have been no legal fees from their own attorney or the thousands of dollars they spent in litigation.

The methods and procedures, legal structure, and GL insurance cost pale in comparison with all that was lost. I hope this story serves as a guide for taking the appropriate measures to protect all assets of significant value. Incident do occur from time to time. Not having protection in place will leave your assets vulnerable, and up for grabs should an accident ensue.

Asset institutions should be equipped with all types of protective mechanisms during the entity construction and operation. The same rules apply for adequate protection in the event of your demise. You cannot achieve this with a sole proprietorship or general partnership structure. Construct your business the right way with longevity in mind.

Form any of the various types of corporations such as S-corporation, C-corporation, B-corporation or registered businesses such as limited partnership, Limited Liability Company or LLC, and finally an estate.

Doing this ensures that no one can go beyond the assets within this entity. Each of the various formation mentioned above has its purpose.

Your business attorney and tax adviser can guide you as to which is appropriate for the type of business you conduct.

Probate Avoidance and Anonymity

The intention is to pursue and acquire assets in the form of businesses that outlives us and is then passed on to our families or beneficiaries. Anyone of the structures mentioned is better than none at all. We don't build businesses and allow thieves and opportunist to take advantage of it. A thriving company with all its protective mechanism already in place defines this philosophy. It should be a mentality of natural reflexes or habit to protect what you've built. Just as most people put on their seat belt when they get in their cars, people should incorporate their business when they establish it. You'll enjoy other benefits of incorporating as well.

An essential document and instrument for making your property anonymous is land trust. Anonymity is a strategy to prevent the public from knowing what assets you own. Building wealth requires a lot of effort and deal making. It takes dedication and sacrifice. Unfortunately, some people exist to pick low hanging fruits. They need a deterrent, and you can give them one by adequately appearing poor while owning and controlling enormous wealth. It is smart, and it gives you peace of mind knowing that your properties are protected.

In the case of any real estate, you can use this instrument to transfer the title of your property to a trustee privately while retaining all the rights to do business as usual with such property. In other words, all your land, residential, and commercial buildings can remain anonymous while you retain the rights to them all. Now when a would-be litigant does an asset search to see if you're worth anything they can go after in the event of a dispute, they see nothing. Not seeing what you're worth means they'll move on to the next victim.

Surely, nobody will spend money and time in a dispute if there's nothing to gain. At least competent attorneys will not take the case on a contingency if they don't see equity anywhere up for grabs.

Living Trust is an effective asset protection tool, and its main purpose is avoiding probate for your family or beneficiary in the event of your demise. Talk to your attorney about establishing a Living Trusts as this document will save your family time and money. There will be no probate court which can take six months to a year and cost lots of money. Your loved ones should focus on other things like properly grieving and reminiscing about the great times, not spending their time in court and wasting their inheritance on attorney fees and unnecessary taxes.

Avoid double taxation of your estate by creating a trust as no tax is deducted on the principal because money entered into the trust is pre-taxed. The one thing you don't want is to build something for your family to inherit and minimize it by failure to plan appropriately. Although the 2017 United States Tax Plan has abolished estate tax, it may be reversed by another president in the future. Your lawyer will know the most current laws surrounding your estate in your area. Most likely, after adding your assets such as life insurance, businesses, stocks, and properties, you'll exceed the threshold of not being taxed. It is therefore important that this aspect is protected as well.

It would be a shame to acquire wealth and lack the ability to protect it. Again, it is essential that you spend the money and have an experienced attorney that specializes in asset protection review your unique circumstances. Such an attorney can design documents to structure entities to minimize liability while maximizing anonymity properly. When correctly executed, your asset protection documents will insulate you from our litigious society.

Take measures to ensure that your wealth successfully transfers to your family, privately and without probate, litigation, or excessive tax. Even your other assets such as 401K, Roth IRA, Life insurance, and others can all be poured into your living trusts at death. By the way, the Roth IRA for your kids can be a partner in one of your real estate LLC and enjoy additional tax benefits but only when the money is used later for college or retirement. If you don't have such intentions, it would not be advantageous to partner your Roth IRA with real estate. Again there's no one size fits all for these types of protection so you must sit down with an experienced lawyer and tax adviser in this field and have them custom design protections for your wealth.

Many in the private finance sector understand that wealth strategies are based on individual goals and therefore, cannot say with one hundred percent certainty about what one must do to build wealth. I can also say that if careful and strategic measures are not taken to protect assets, it can all vanish within a short period. It is therefore smart with the help of your team to formulate a system that protects your assets well beyond your own life and the next generations to come.

General liability protects the insured from losing their assets in the event someone is injured or suffer a loss associated with your assets. In most circumstances, damages caused or affiliated with your assets can be mitigated by the general liability insurance coverage. In such cases, the insurance settles with the subject, and you continue with business as usual.

Not having this insurance and facing the same scenario means either coming up with a monetary cure or possibly being forced to sell your asset in order to settle. The latter is not desirable to an asset owner, so adequate general liability insurance is one way to prevent this from ever occurring.

When you have children or other people whose life and well-being is your responsibility, life insurance is a must. It simply takes care of them in the event of your demise. The financial burden of food, clothing shelter education, healthcare, and others can all be taken care of with the proceeds from life insurance. A beneficiary simply files a claim, and the insurance company confirms the death by verifying a few documents. Upon proof that the insured is no longer alive, the total amount insured is remitted to the beneficiaries.

Life insurance can be purchased on your own behalf or for others with their approval. Whoever purchases the policy is the owner and therefore pays the premium. The insured is the person whom the policy is written.

The policy itself is a contract stipulating terms of agreement such as the amount and beneficiaries etc. The two types of life insurance are term and permanent. Some of the difference is that term is designed to benefit others when you die while permanent allows you to use some of the matured money when needed.

Term is cheaper while permanent carries a higher premium. It is also worth to note that term is cheap because it has no savings component like permanent does.

"Even the lion, the king of the forest, protects himself against flies." - Ghanaian proverb

CHAPTER SIX:

Teach Your Children to Pursue Assets Early

The moment to teach your children about assets is now. Think about it. You teach your children core values and life skills. They learn how to walk and talk emulating family members. You teach them how to share and many other social and economic skills like budgeting and being financially responsible. It is time to teach your children to pursue assets. They should know that working for an employer for a lifetime should not be their agenda. A lifetime as an employee without seeking any assets of their own is not the best way to thrive financially.

The only exception will be if they belong to an elite group of people that makes up less than 1% of the population. The rest must understand why it is essential to pursue assets early.

They must understand the difference between assets and liabilities. They should know to buy enough assets until it begins to produce sufficient income to surpass their lifestyle expenses.

When you teach your children about assets, it closes the wealth gap, and there's nothing better than success duplication from you. More light will be shed upon this basic premise in this chapter.

The Approach

Teach your children that they are an asset. Tell them everyone is an asset because we all have the earning potential. Your very existence and whatever physical, mental, spiritual capabilities you possess are all tools that can be utilized to acquire more assets. To properly use the tools that you already possess, one must have a clear understanding of who they are, what they seek to achieve, and how to bring it into fruition. When these factors are properly defined, one would have already begun on the journey of financial education. The key is to realize that you are an asset, and you must decide to acquire more assets. Even the person that has no money, no job, and no savings are just as much of an asset as the person that has much more.

Asset is anyone or anything of value. Anyone can be hired, contracted, or utilized to help create more value, and anything of value can be acquired solely to generate more value. At an absolute minimum, asset is the person or thing that has the potential of generating value that can be converted into continuous supply of money or cash flow as I use the terms interchangeably. Therefore, no matter what your circumstances may be, your trajectory is already destined to make money, and that is the purpose of an asset. If you're not satisfied with how much money you make, then you will have to tap into the other assets mentioned above. The concept of getting more assets is simple, but it must truly resonate with you before proceeding — measures to protect your assets before you get it and beyond will be explained throughout the subsequent chapters.

An asset in its simplest form consists of two factors. These two factors, when properly understood, will make a big difference going forward. I will explain. In the paragraph above, I mentioned that asset makes you money. What if your first asset does not make sufficient money to meet your goal? Well, you will have to buy more assets. The more assets you utilize or acquire, the more money you generate. If becoming wealthy is your desire, it makes no sense to take on liabilities. Exhaust every option possible to use debt in all your asset acquisition with the exception of a down payment or administration cost.

Look at it this way; asset is the total of liabilities and equity. Liabilities are what you owe, a negative number, and equity is what you own, a positive number. In fact, with the exception of shelter, food, clothing, transportation, utilities and a few other essential things for your family, which are all liabilities, everything else that you buy should be an asset if you intend on becoming and staying wealthy. Equity is nice, but always acquire assets that produce cash flow. Teach your children that an asset that does not produce cash flow should be sold for one that does.

More often than not, those that say all their bills are necessities and therefore have no allowance to buy assets may have a change of heart after careful examination of their lifestyle. Even those that maintain that money wasted is insignificant, after having exposure of what it could have become, may also rethink their position. The fact remains that money spent on liabilities die immediate death and therefore never grows. Money invested in assets; however, have a great probability of growing and sometimes exponentially if done intelligently.

Teach Asset and Close Wealth Gap

The subject of asset is not taught in school or at home enough to resonate in the minds of children.

Pursuit of ~~Happiness~~ Assets

Just ask a group of school children what they wish to do as adults and they all most likely point to doing a job as an employee. They'll say, lawyer, doctor or other specialized professions. Some may say a job in the skilled trade category, while a few will lean towards becoming an athletic star or an entertainer.

All of those professions are okay, but those that wish to use it as a tool in acquiring assets will prosper well above the others.

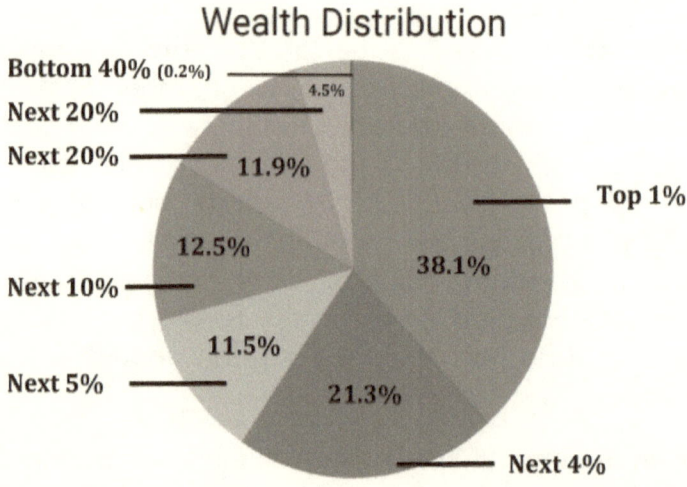

Let's take the lawyer for an example. It is a professional asset that can be transformed or use as a gateway to more assets. I'll explain. The average salary of a lawyer is close to that of the middle class. If he or she begins to buy liabilities such a big home, an expensive car, jewelry, and other extravagant things, remaining funds may be too small to purchase assets. The better approach would be to live moderately and obtain assets, and in due time, those assets will generate the proceeds necessary to live a plush life. Some of the proceeds can be allocated to help the less fortunate.

Even though I used an attorney to illustrate my point, anyone from any profession can make strides towards pursuing assets. It is not limited to only the middle class or the rich. Poor people can also use what they have to get what they want. In fact, they may be able to live below their means more effectively. Determined people who earn less, may get there faster with a thorough understanding of how to leverage specialized knowledge, credit, and other assets. No matter how low you sit economically, the right knowledge and using the dislike of your circumstances as a motivation to transform your life should be a top agenda.

Teach your children about assets, money, and credit. In doing so, they'll get it right much earlier than others.

They will understand that while it's ok to get a job, it is more rewarding to be a business owner and an investor.

They should know that having an abundant life should be used for the good of humankind. Teaching, helping, and creating opportunities are all things that are needed by others who are less fortunate. In essence, they'll be proficient in identifying things of value and importance. It is, therefore, no brainer that they'll seek more things of value. These children would be more susceptible to helping others because of how they think and see the world is largely based on foundations at school and at home.

When children speak of becoming an employee and nothing else, it is a result of indoctrination which failed to give attention to assets. They simply don't understand or even care too much for it. The wealth gap, however, would close significantly if adults teach their children important subjects like assets. All the types and how to convert it into cash continually should be properly understood by the time a child graduate middle or junior high school. The shift will manifest itself when more children begin to say I want to be a business owner or an investor.

For most people, working a financially comfortable job is good enough. These people have no problem whatsoever being an employee. There's nothing wrong with this philosophy if you have true security and equity in the employer. Unfortunately, there's very little true security in working for someone else. From a low-level technician to the CEO of a fortune 500 company, job security is not guaranteed. This is the reason why I emphasize making a shift from an employee to an employer. When you become an employer, your future is in your hands. You reap the benefits of your hard work.

Understand that any resource that has potential value is an asset and how it is used is a major factor in reaching one's goal of creating wealth. This is the reason why an old rundown building that is boarded up with do not trespass signs, can be rebuilt or repurposed for vitality and profit.

Similarly, an old shopping strip or structure when renovated can be worth much more. Assets are far from being limited to real estate. Almost any asset used effectively can produce an attractive profit. The key is to be able to identify assets from liabilities. Most people are still confused by the difference with the exception of the obvious.

It's About Your Legacy

You've reached a point where you know what is working and what isn't. Do more of what's working. Elevate it for higher returns, expand it to bigger profits, and fine tune it, so it produces a better efficiency. Once you are able to measure and quantify your return on investments, whether it's from profits, passive income or dividends, you will be in a position to make decisions on which areas to duplicate and the direction of your legacy. Repeat what brings you the most return on investments. Continue to grow your wealth. Be sure to pay it forward as you begin to accumulate wealth as many are less fortunate than we are. The importance of networking is emphasized again because working with the best is indispensable. My Devise Wealth Mastermind Facebook Group is the best place to meet and network with a like-minded group of people that are building wealth with online/offline businesses, real estate, and investments.

There comes a time where innovation is necessary. Those that refuse when the environments dictate adaptation are sure to fail. Duplicating success involves paying attention to your business and staying ahead of trends. It also requires seeking growth periodically. A successful online business that sells affiliate products can venture into creating and selling its own products. Let's say your business sells apparel merchandise. At some point, looking into having your own brand of merchandise is not far-fetched. In fact, it should be part of your overall business plan. I'm not insinuating that you abandon the other products, but rather add your brand to such products.

You are already selling similar items; therefore, integrating your products is a great way to expand. This act is seen across all sectors of commerce. Almost all grocery stores carry their own brand. If you pay attention, you will find that lots of restaurants carry their own brand of condiments and snacks, among others. The list goes on, but I think you get the idea. Being open to new ideas makes us better, and the same is expected of our businesses.

A real estate business that buys and rent single-family homes at some point should venture into apartment complexes. Single-family homes are an excellent way to build wealth because of the potential of equity, cash flow, tax savings in the form of depreciation, repairs, and improvement. It is not volatile and can be sold to recoup your investment within a few months. My students that venture into single-family rental homes are doing turnkey, which is great. It is the next progression to venture into apartment complexes. You are more than likely not experienced enough, or maybe even lack the resources to be part of an apartment complex acquisition when you first start. Soon you will be.

There are greater rewards with commercial properties. First, the entire property is in one place and managed by one property management company. It's multi-units, and if the property management is good, your average occupancy should be around 95%. This means that you should have a great net operating income or NOI. The net operating income is the number you get when you subtract your operating expense from gross operating income. Of course, you have to factor in mortgage and insurance, etc., to determine your cash flow. In a nutshell, all the benefits of a single-family rental is the same with apartment complexes, but at a greater level.

Increasing the dollar amount of your investments that have done well for a number of years is a sound act if all the indicators remain the same. To build substantial wealth with investment, the shares have to increase in value, and you have to invest continually for some time. An investment of $200 a month in mutual funds that averages an interest of 10% yearly will earn you three million dollars in fifty years. Just imagine what would happen if you double your investment. Starting early and staying consistent is the key to growing your wealth through investment. One day, you'll hand over all your assets to your loved ones. Teach the same to your children to ensure they honor your legacy

"The young bird does not crow until it hears the old ones."
- Tswana proverb

SECTION III

Asset Power Moves: What and How?

Be aware that we have a limited amount of real and natural assets. They can be found on, above, and below the ground. Acquire real estate and do what's necessary to make your business operate with or without your presence, while allocating time for other investments. When you reach the level of determining what key asset to pursue, all decisions should be based on prospect of the asset for at least the next few decades.

The following questions must produce satisfactory answers. Have I done adequate research on the asset? Is there a great demand for this asset? What is my business plan and unique selling proposition or USP? Who are my customers? Is this a profitable asset type? How will I market this asset? What is the risk involved? Do I have the team needed? Is there adequate financing available? Are there tax reduction benefits? Finally, do I have an exit strategy?

You must structure the best protection for your asset.

Pursuit of ~~Happiness~~ Assets

The types of protection varies however some essentials are official address, a corporate attorney, entity structuring, license and permits, insurance, tax accountant and an easy to follow system of operation.

In the next three chapters, we will examine some of the best assets to consider and how to go about it. Real and natural assets are of limited quantity so the value will continue to rise until the end of times.

Others are at least as infinite as your imagination and creativity in the foreseeable future.

CHAPTER SEVEN:

Real Estate Above and Below Ground

As you focus on the surface of the land, bear in mind, there may be a significant value above and below the ground in real estate. It is especially true in mineral-rich deposit zone areas. There may be above ground profits for cities where adjacent buildings need air space. First, let's look underneath.

In some cases, the minerals or fossils found below the ground may be more valuable than the land or structure itself. Imagine if oil, diamond, gold, or other valuables are discovered under your property. This would be a game changer because you are entitled to it all, as long as it's stipulated in your purchase agreement.

There may be cases as well, where big pay will be given for air space around a building. This has occurred in major cities in the past. I cited an instance in chapter one, where this very thing occurred. It happened at Christ Church in New York where apparently, the owners of that building sold its air space rights for over $30 million. There are others, so seeing an opportunity of mutual benefit and seizing is what it's all about. We'll explore real estate asset and strategies to attain them.

Single Family One to Four Units

Real estate on the residential level is the most needed as everyone needs a safe, secure, and workable shelter. In the United States, one to four units are considered residential while anything five or more are regarded as commercial. Regardless of classification, the prospect for housing is great, and many lack qualifications for ownership. It is also expensive for most people to buy, so they tend to rent. As a result, the demand for real estate continues to rise for all these centuries. On the other hand, some take out loans and later default for one reason or another.

There are also folks that fail to pay their taxes on their real estate. Some are also faced with expensive repair cost of upkeep that they cannot afford. The point that I'm conveying here is that whether a person faces foreclosure, tax liens, or other forms of hardship, you can provide a way out for them and make profit in the process. You can do it for single family, duplex, triplex and four-plex on the residential side and five or more as commercial.

It's about lessening their burden by paying their liabilities and acquiring their property at a discount in exchange. After all, the purpose of acquiring properties is to profit, so helping someone out of debt and being compensated is a viable asset pursuit. To do it, you must look to buy substantially below market value. This is especially so if you intend on repairing and selling or fix and flip as it is commonly referred. Let's be clear; you are simply marketing directly to property owners that may need a financial rescue. You're basically identifying and solving a problem that others have either overlooked or haven't noticed. In fact, being a problem solver is a great way to help people and earn compensation. It is being done one property at a time in real estate.

If making a substantial profit one property at a time is not your goal, renting is another option that can produce monthly cash flow. Start by actively looking for distressed homeowners. These owners are delinquent on their mortgage payment or taxes and want a way out. Your purpose is to help them get out without ruining their credit. Most of them may downgrade into an apartment or move in with a family member. Make an offer to pay their delinquent balance or taxes, give them some agreed upon money and take over the mortgage payment. Make sure the owner has adequate equity or else don't do the deal.

If you are a first-time home buyer, your focus should be a duplex, triplex, or a four-plex. You may be required to live there for at least a year so live in one and rent the rest. The multi-family unit gives you the leverage of paying your mortgage with your tenant's money and having excess cash flow. If you don't like the idea of living with your tenant, move out, and rent your portion after one year. You may find a residential rental property to be quite beneficial, but time-consuming as you acquire more and more. In that case, you can turn to turnkey solutions. There are companies that does the entire process from finding to closing on a property. They even do any repairs needed, rent the property, and manage it as well. These turkey home providers usually charge a ten percent management fee.

Multifamily Five Units or More

There are many forms of commercial real estate with each having its own pros and cons. Among some of the more profitable ones are multi-family units such as apartment complexes. If the multifamily units are more than four, it's commercial. There are other commercial units such as office buildings, shopping mall, hotels, strip centers, mobile home parks, and storage units. All of these properties are profitable and can accelerate your wealth dramatically. For starters with no experience, as always, your first assignment is to educate yourself on the subject. There are real estate investment groups known as crowdfunding. Perhaps you can start there as you learn the ropes and become more familiar. This option is preferred initially because the entry point is significantly low. With as little as five thousand dollars, you can own a part of the investment and receive all the data that pertain to it. Doing it this way will give you a chance to use what you've learned against real data from your investment.

Proceed to collect cash distribution from income and appreciation and gain more experience before looking into acquiring your own property. Even then, you should partner with an experienced investor before buying one entirely on your own. All these precautions and learning on the job or LOJ should be taken to avoid expensive mistakes. It is better to do multiple ventures with experienced investors than do one on your own if you're inexperienced. After one or two ventures, or when you've gained sufficient experience in commercial real estate deals, go for it. Proceed to a sole acquisition.

You need a good team when you decide to buy your own

property. Among them are an experienced mentor or consultant, commercial real estate agents and brokers, Lenders, Lawyer, Accountant, Appraiser, property management company, and a good assistant. All members of your team should have experience. Your mentor or consultant should also recommend them. This type of acquisition requires a lot of due diligence by a reputable and experienced team. You will have to physically examine tens of properties and analyze numbers before buying one.

When you study commercial real estate investing, you'll quickly become familiar with factors such as submarket cap rate, price per unit (door), Expenses per unit (door), and rent for one, two and three bedrooms. You'll be able to take a look at comparable sales data and break it down. Other factors like net operating income or NOI, cash on cash return or COCR, sometimes referred to as ROI, and debt coverage ratio or DCR will be properly understood. Looking at properties and seeing the potential will become second nature. You'll know the right questions to ask in regards to making a ready cost, occupancy, evictions, and other tenant-related questions.

After the results of due diligence indicates a good deal, take a loan from the bank and acquire the real estate property. Rent the property, and your tenants will pay the mortgage. You'll have surplus money for yourself after the mortgage payment. You see, when you're in this position, lenders will give you seventy to seventy-five percent of the funds needed to buy the property. With just about thirty percent, you're now the owner of the entire property. As soon as you can rent the property however, you no longer have to use your own money to pay the mortgage. This is a classic example of using debt to acquire wealth. Using debt or other people's money to acquire assets that produce cash flow is a mindset of the wealthy. Do not forsake this mindset.

In the example given above, the bank, in essence, is the mastermind because they loan other people's money to serious, credible people and institutions and collect an attractive interest while giving the depositors of money the absolute minimum in interest. Taking a loan to buy assets is like taking a play out of the bank's playbook. As I've mentioned over again, repeat all substantially profitable ventures. This strategy is clever and takes a life of its own as you continue to accelerate your wealth. The more asset acquisition you partake, the more your net worth grows, meaning the bigger profits you earn.

Other benefits of commercial real estate is appreciation. An investment in this type of property is certainly going to appreciate over time. If you decide to sell it after a few years, the value would have increased. The extent of the increase depends on comparable sales data for the area or submarket as well as improvements made to the property. It is not far-fetched to buy a property, do some repairs, add improvements, and increase the value by at least twenty-five to fifty percent. Experienced investors in this field can identify properties with such an upside, as it is called.

When you decide to sell a commercial real estate property, you can buy a bigger one, and all the taxes are deferred. It is called a 1031 exchange. This is an IRS code that allows an investor to acquire a more expensive property or one with more units after selling a previous one without paying taxes on it. There are a few rules that must be followed, such as the timeframe between the sale and acquisition as well as the value between the two properties. This is important for building wealth because you want to avoid liabilities everywhere you can.

Apart from the appreciation of commercial real estate assets, there are numerous other very important benefits. Among them is depreciation. It is expected that a property has a useful life of 27.5 years, according to the IRS. Consequently, you'll have a lower tax liability in the form of tax savings each year. We all understand that a property wears out over time and that depreciation translates to tax deductions.

After owning a cash producing property for a couple of years with an appreciation in value and equity, the entire process can be repeated. Members of your team, especially your real estate agents and brokers, are going to be constantly presenting properties to you. A good team will know what you like. Therefore, they will filter through and only offer what fits your style. When you find another deal that produces cash flow, has an upside, and meet your requirements, you can buy and increase your assets.

The same strategies can be used to acquire other related commercial real estate properties such as office building and shopping strips etc. Be advised that each type is a little different, and therefore, the key to success is education. Immerse yourself in learning and due diligence before purchasing any real estate. As mentioned previously, start small and gain some experience before going big.

A must have investment is the acquisition of rental commercial real estate property such as apartment complex, office building, hotels, shopping mall, high rise building, or storage building. Again, a team would be needed to vet the details of the property, complete the deal, and manage the property. In any case, if done properly with essential systems and processes previously discussed, your wealth will only continue to grow to a delightful net worth. A yearly evaluation of your assets along with your team will let you know when to make the next move.

Commercial real estate is a tremendous overall asset area for wealth building, and the most stable of them all is apartment complexes. Many benefits come with real estate investments such as low out of pocket investments because most lenders will lend up to seventy-five percent of the sale price. Think about it, the control and management of a multi-million-dollar property, and you only invest up to twenty-five percent. Meanwhile, the total cost of the project is credited to you since you own the mortgage. It opens greater doors and places you in other exclusive networks.

You will certainly enjoy appreciation as well as depreciation benefits. With appreciation, it is partly a natural thing that occurs with real estate due to economic factors. The other part is forced appreciation. If appropriately trained, however, you can acquire properties with an upside and instantly increase the appreciation by a large amount. Let's say you buy a property that needs some improvement or upgrades. You spent capital to do the renovation. Upon completion, you will increase rent on each unit. Remember, net operating income is income minus expense. The rise in rent will cause your NOI to increase and therefore, instant value appreciation. When this occurs, depreciation, which is a tax deduction, will increase as well because it is based on the value over a twenty-seven years period. Keep in mind that improvement has to be cost-effective so that there is a cash flow increase when the expenses are factored in.

You can even do a 1031 exchange when you buy a bigger or more expansive property without paying any taxes. The premise of doing this transaction is that you don't just sell the property. You sell to acquire another one. Usually, you'll sell to acquire a bigger property or a more profitable property. Regardless of what you buy, it must be done within a specific amount of time and requirements. Among some of the guidelines are the same taxpayer doing the swap and up to six months maximum time to complete. Tax is a liability and takes money out of your pocket. Money that can be invested in other assets, so it is good to defer it through this exchange. The most important of all the benefits of real estate investment is cash flow. When due diligence is done correctly, you can acquire a property that will cash flow positively from month one, after the deal is complete.

Commercial real estate is very broad. Aside from any 5 or more multifamily units, other structures such as office buildings, shopping mall, hotels, strip centers, mobile home parks, and storage units belong to this classification.

Although these are all real estate, specific experience in doing deals in each one is recommended for optimal success. One way to achieve that is to join forces with people that have a track record of success. Perhaps having basic knowledge of how each one works is needed but not to be substituted with having the overall experience of a team.

Commercial real estate is obviously more expensive, therefore minimizing or avoiding rookie mistakes could be the difference between failed and successful venture.

When you gain the knowledge and experience, you can utilize it as an asset, and bring investors in for a deal of mutual benefits. This process in real estate is known as syndication. With this method, a person can be part owner of a real estate acquisition without using any of his or her own money. It's all about how your syndication is constructed. It's a type of crowdfunding as you'll raise the capital from tens, hundreds, or even thousands of people who want to make real estate investment without being active. This deal can yield attractive returns sometimes better than average stocks. There are other benefits as well, such as equity and depreciation. The mere fact of using leverage to control a property and get all these benefits is phenomenal when compared to other investments.

The key thing is to follow the rules of the Security and exchange commission or other government institutions that governs securities around the world. This area is a requirement that cannot be neglected. Anyone without an experienced team may very well be over their heads. Syndication requires deep understanding in various sectors pertaining to it, such as law, tax accounting, financing, property evaluation, and management.

People who choose to be part of syndication should thoroughly vet the company before giving them money. Although many laws govern securities, you are ultimately responsible for protecting yourself and your investments.

"Buy real estate in areas where the path exists and buy more real estate where there is no path, but you can create your own." - David Waronker

CHAPTER EIGHT:

Turn-key & Strategic Business Alliances

When it comes to building turnkey strategic business alliances, there are many factors at play and multiple moving parts. The ability to coordinate them well determines your success. The goal to doing this is to design or purchase systems that once activated minimizes your future efforts. These systems must be turnkey and strategic as the name implies and easy for even unskilled people to follow. Of course, you'll work with skillful people; however, simplicity makes continuity possible and replacement of human resource when necessary seamless. In this chapter, we'll identify what types of assets are profitable, yet easy to accomplish these said factors.

Systems

Building wealth requires systems for generating multiple streams of income. Make a deliberate attempt to acquire an asset that has such potential. Systems should be asset specific

Pursuit of ~~Happiness~~ Assets

but nonetheless applicable to any industry of interest. No matter what asset you pursue, it must be equipped with processes that makes its operation simple. The days of "Jack of all trades" are long gone. Virtually every aspect of your asset should be capable of being outsources to someone else. As you will discover in chapter 13, a leader has to visualize what needs to be done, but a manager sees to it that it's done. Most people start out playing both roles and may even be part of the workforce as well. The idea is to separate yourself from these duties and focus on making the asset optimal. Keep this in mind when building your assets.

If you are buying an existing asset, make sure it has these attributes or can easily be converted to include them. The end product should be turnkey with strategic business alliances so as you scale up and hire more staff; you are able to remove yourself from working in the company entirely. You can accomplish much more when your time is dedicated to making the overall asset better rather than doing the day to day tedious function of the workforce.

As part of the overall system of generating wealth, multiple streams of income should be at the forefront. A set up that allows various built-in ways of earning income re-enforces the structure and hence more cash flow. Not having it is basically putting all your eggs in one basket. It is not wise as there's no absolute certainty. We take calculated risk based on education and understanding of the product or service as well as the historical performances and trends. Other indicators include evaluation, quality, demand, due diligence, vision, and an experienced, competent team to execute. These elements minimize unforeseen problems that could slow the progress of the wealth building process.

Having multiple streams of income establishes a comfort zone that enables branching into other ventures. It safeguards against industry fluctuations and works as a hedge when a downturn occurs in certain areas. All the same, it increases net worth and opens more doors into bigger ventures and acquisitions. The groundwork takes time and precision, but if done correctly, there are many benefits to enjoy.

Some areas that are a must include online and offline business, real estate, and paper asset investments. There are so many profitable opportunities in these areas for those that have the knowledge, experience, and the team. In a lot of cases, these areas can be artificially inter-connected depending on the specific product or service. Build your business with the type of thinking that everything must be installed on the surface of real estate.

The case for the real estate itself and offline business is certainly plain to see, but the same holds true for online business. It is a virtual real estate with billions of potential customers. The cost to have a piece of it can be zero or at your own set price. You read it right. There are many opportunities for making consistent money online without a website, software, ads, or any other tools that otherwise would cost money. The business-savvy, however, would quickly graduate it into a structure with systems of wealth that requires some capital investment.

As online, there are no shortages of profitable options for offline businesses. It takes a lot more capital in most cases to construct. The mentality should not be about how much it takes necessarily but the earning potential of the business. Getting the resources needed would not be difficult if the business plan is comprehensive and demonstrates profitability. With money credit and leverage, the business is likely to get funded. For these reasons, asking how much can be made is a better question, as opposed to how much is the cost.

Whenever possible, the offline business should include ownership of the building. Try to avoid leasing a space to operate. Paying someone else mortgage while they enjoy all the tax benefits, appreciation, and cash flow is not something to take great pleasure in. Constructing or buying your own building increases your net worth, and affords you all the benefits mentioned above, in addition to your business itself. It's the best way to approach an offline business. Owning the real estate in which you operate simply adds many other benefits and value to the business like no other.

Your streams of income are incomplete without rental real estate. It is always good to start with a single family, duplex, triplex, or fourplex. Starting off by collecting multiple rental incomes increases the cash flow while still yielding to all the other benefits mentioned above. The equity will also grow much faster-allowing access to more capital for expansion into bigger units. Even when the economy is not as strong, people will still need a place to stay so the demand would be more stable.

Paper asset investment should not be overlooked. As with other investment, research must be conducted to identify the best paper assets to buy. Getting in early is also very important because the value can become too diluted for any real significant gains if the company later lack innovation. Profitable paper assets such as stocks produces dividends which can be re-deposited into buying more stocks or simply cashed out. There is no particular set rule when it comes to the type of online, offline, real estate, or paper asset investment in particular. Overall, it should be something you know and understand. It should also be profitable. Always use arbitrage when deciding what type of business to start or acquire.

Networking

Networking allows you to see through other people's lenses. You would be shocked at what you find in terms of opportunities when you make an effort to pay attention to potential assets. Make it part of your routine to talk and network with people. When you dine at a franchise restaurant or order takeout, chances are the owner of that restaurant is not actually working there.

In most cases, the entire establishment is operated using systems that any manager and staff follows to achieve success. This turnkey business can be duplicated over and over again. Many owners usually have multiple locations because it is much easier to repeat what works than to start something new. After all, there's brand recognition, proven systems, and ultimately profitability.

Sometimes it may also be a matter of convenience. We are living in the age and time where more people demand healthier foods on the go. People also enjoy having a place to hold informal business and student group meetings. Location is once again a maker or a breaker. My advice is to pick an area with close proximity to downtown, a major university, or a busy business strip.

The food has to be good and friendly staff often makes a big difference. Convenience is also key since many among the working class are constantly on the go. Pricing should be competitive, and quality must be a top priority. Take it a step further by adding complimentary internet connection hotspot. With an increase in the population being conscious of their health and well-being, having a healthier section on the menu is not a bad idea.

Fossil deposits and the likes are a great means of energy, and finding a way to produce and use it responsibly is the duty of all humankind who understands its effect. Continued innovation in this sector is needed to make sure we leave a better tomorrow environmentally for generations to come. If fossil deposits like oil and coal cannot be extracted and use without harming the environment, then an alternative such as wind and solar energy from the sun should be explored on a massive scale.

As we all know, the power of the sun in our solar system can totally replace all the fossils fuels we currently use without any harmful effects to our planet. There are massive opportunities not only in the equipment technology but also storage, distribution, and the technical side of it.

Solar technology from direct sunlight and wind is still in its infancy. The potential is huge, especially in Africa, where the continent has more direct exposure to sunlight than the remaining continents. Companies that put resources into this sector are sure to win in a big way.

Before signing any endorsement contract, think strategic business alliance. This approach will be beneficial in multiple ways. Many people of celebrity status often endorse a product without taking care of the business side of the endorsement. If you are a star or have a large following, take the time to educate yourself to ensure your deals are fair before signing any contract. It does not make sense to endorse a product and reap benefits at a minuscule level.

Know your worth, and negotiate well. Whenever possible, ask for equity as well as distribution. Audit the proceeds from your endorsement periodically or the valuation to see the whole picture. Although your agent will do all these tasks, it is good to be in the know, so you're not ripped off.

"SUCCESSFUL PEOPLE DO WHAT UNSUCCESSFUL PEOPLE ARE NOT WILLING TO DO. DON'T WISH IT WERE EASIER; WISH YOU WERE BETTER." - *Jim Rohn*

CHAPTER NINE:

Stocks & Bonds Diversification

Diversification in stocks goes far beyond just spreading your investments across multiple asset classes. They must be invested in uncorrelated asset classes. This is a true way to avoid being significantly impacted by market volatility. For example, when one asset class is moving up, instead of another moving down, there's no effect. When what happens to one has no effect whatsoever to another, you have successfully diversified.

This subject is often misunderstood as many simply buy assets from different industries or of different size and call it a day. Some think buying, for example, a technology stock and a financial stock makes it diversified. The problem with that thinking is that there are factors that can cause a correlation between both assets. Besides, both are a form of security.

Buying equities and commodities is a true example of diversification. Since equities are long term assets in nature and commodities are short term, what happens to one has zero correlation to the other.

In this chapter, we'll take a closer look at the stock market. Its purpose and a brief history will be disclosed. You'll know what key indicators to watch when investing in the stock market and how to evaluate them. You will have a keen sense of what to analyze before investing.

We'll also take a closer look at bonds and mutual funds as these are a large portion of the market.

The Stock Market

Another profitable way of owning parts or shares of other businesses is by participating in the stock market. It is a place where trading takes place between buyers and sellers. When it first began in the 16th century in Europe, all trading was done at a physical location called the stock exchange. Today there are many stock exchanges such as New York, London, Tokyo, Chicago, Shanghai, and hundreds more, however with the emergence of the internet, most trading are now conducted electronically. You can literally sit at home on your computer, laptop, or even a smartphone, set up an account online, make a deposit, and begin trading. In fact, it has never been easier to buy or sell a stock.

To put this into context, there are at least 60 major stock exchanges in the world. The total value in terms of revenue is about $69 trillion. Of the total revenue, 16 exchanges belong to the trillion dollars exclusive club. This simply means they have an asset of one trillion dollars or more. Collectively, these 16 exchanges control 87% of the market capitalization. The remaining 44 smaller ones still control billions of dollars each with a total of $9 trillion. By far the largest in America is the New York stock exchange. Japan Exchange Group is the largest in Asia. As far as Europe, the biggest is Euronext. Johannesburg Stock Exchange is the largest in Africa, but others include Egyptian and Nigerian Stock Exchange.

When a company has done relatively well and wants to expand, rather than using its own money or applying for a loan for expansion, it may elect to sell some of its shares to raise the money. Before it can do such a thing, it must make a transition from a privately owned to a publicly owned company, by filing documents with security and exchange commission (SEC) in the United States, or it's equivalent in other countries. This act is called Initial public offering or IPO. The company will decide how many shares it's willing to sell and open it up to the stock market. The public, whether a person or an entity can now buy stocks or shares in that business entity, making each buyer a part owner.

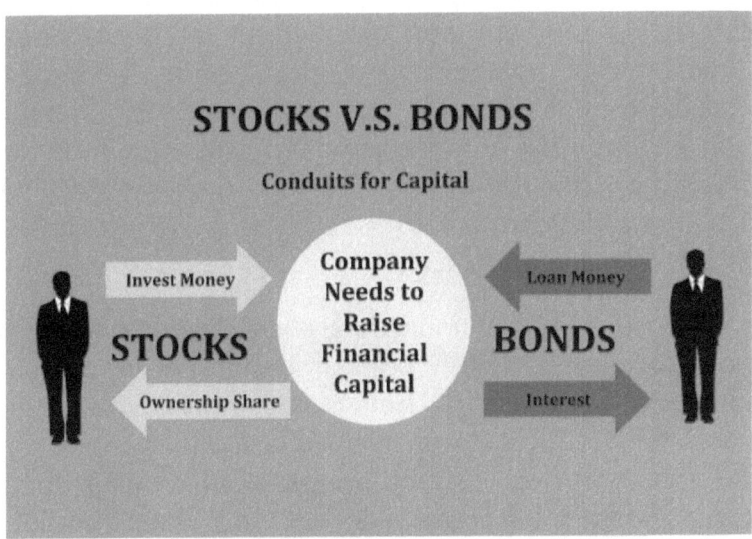

Usually, companies engage in a pre-IPO before going public. This closed-door transaction is exclusive to private equity firms, hedge funds, angel or sophisticated investors. Since its private, knowing the right people places you in a position to make this early investment. The pre-IPO investors usually get much better terms and opportunity to earn more. The amount per share is usually discounted for these early birds that help the company in raising money.

Everyone else comes in as an investor when a company finally goes public. People and institutions purchase stocks with the expectations that the value will increase over time. If it does, you can sell and make a profit. Stocks prices are forever changing due to market dictations, and people are always buying and selling so a typical stock in the course of a day will fluctuate by the minute from opening to closing of the stock market.

Before buying shares in any company, however, there must be some research to make sure the company is worth its valuation, financially sound, has great leadership and vision and it has a steady history of growth and value. Intrinsic value is the actual value, not the market value of an asset or a company. To evaluate intrinsic value properly, you must fundamentally examine both qualitative and quantitative aspects. This means that you have to look at management and its model as well as the amount of cash flow it has. The subject of knowing how to read a financial statement is once again raised because it is essential to be able to do so.

An investor will look at indicators such as price to earnings ratio or P/E, and previously paid dividends. As always, there's no substitute for education before you enter a new area of business. Also, education on the subject and working with a mentor that has had success in the stock market is highly advisable. Read publications like The Wall Street Journal and Investor's Business Daily. You can also learn the ins-and-outs of trading at investopedia.com. There are many financial services institutions that work as intermediaries between the trader and the stock market.

When you are ready to dive in, search for online discount brokers and look for ones that are well established with high ratings and low commission fees. Be sure to get a written disclosure of all fees before you sign up. Some of the top firms include Merrill Lynch, Charles Schwab, Fidelity, Vanguard and E-Trade. Vanguard is one of the largest investment companies in the world. It manages over 4.5 Trillion dollars in assets.

Buying Debt AKA Bonds

Bonds are investment tool opposite from stock in that it is simply buying debt. A company or a government can issue bonds, meaning debt that is promised to be paid at a future date. It is a loan that is borrowed from the public, and certificates are issued to validate it. The certificate indicates a maturity date, interest rate, and a dollar amount to be paid. A bond certificate holder will receive their interest on their money a couple of times a year until it reached a maturity date. At that time, the original amount of money invested is returned to the bondholder.

If you want to invest in bonds, you should know a few things about the borrower. For instance, can this borrower pay back the money? What is their track record of paying debts? What is their credit rating? What are the funds going to be used for and a host of other important answers? In a way, you must have a similar approach that lenders have towards you when you apply for a loan or credit. After all, when one lends money, they expect to be repaid on time and with interest.

Bonds are just another strategy a nation or corporation uses to raise capital. They use these funds to operate the business, expand, or acquire other business. In most cases, they will pay you higher interest than what a bank pays, so people have more to gain from bonds than leaving their money in a savings account. The company, at the same time, enjoys paying less interest to bondholders than they would pay if they borrowed from banks. As a result, it appears like a win-win for all parties.

Do keep in mind that as with any investment, you can lose

everything if the company goes into default. Though rare, this can certainly happen. They key is doing your research to make sure the company has a solid financial statement and steady growth history as other indicators. When you decide to make an investment of any kind, you should always consult with your financial adviser for his or her professional insight.

Mutual funds

The concept of pooling money together from investors to buy securities such as stocks and bonds, commodities, real estate, and other assets is known as mutual funds. The company pays dividends in the form of distribution but does not grant voting rights to its investors. This method has been around for hundreds of years, and more than $17 trillion of security assets are held in mutual funds.

It's a long-term strategy plan managed professionally and typically has lower transaction cost than other securities.

There are so many strategies and asset classes for mutual funds. Although most people invest in hopes of a rising market, there are other options. One such option operates, so gains are realized from a falling market.

This structure is known as a bear market. Mutual fund is similar to stocks; however, selling may not take place until the end of the day. On the bright side, transaction costs are lower than that of stocks.

"Where you will sit when you are old shows where you stood in youth". - Yoruba proverb

SECTION IV

Asset Power Moves: Where and How?

There are no short of opportunities in any city, state or province. A careful evaluation will reveal many areas where one can provide a solution to a problem for the masses anywhere in the world. You must consider the fact that the emergence of technology has now made it possible to operate virtually anywhere on the habitable globe. The limits people and organizations faced decades ago are now for the most part things of the past. Many assets pursuit can now occur globally, and local control is very much viable.

Here are a few questions that must be answered in terms of where to pursue assets.

Are there any guarantees as far as safety stability and security is concerned? Where is technology heading and how can I stay in the forefront of the trends? These important questions must be answered to assure confidence in your selections.

In this section, we are going to explore where and how to pursue assets. You will see how the barriers that once existed are now artificial and no longer physical. Technology improvements in transportation, communication, commerce and transaction have made it all possible to pursue assets where there's opportunity for great profits

CHAPTER TEN:

Opportunities in Your Region

With the ability to think differently, a trained person in any field can identify and evaluate opportunities that pique their interest. There's an abundant amount of sectors and sub-sectors of our thriving economy. Everyone does not have to pursue the same type of assets. The options one chooses often derives from familiarity, interest, training, and earning potential. At other times, people would rather stick to the asset type they understand because it makes the pursuit more comfortable.

This notion is quite alright, but one should always weigh the opportunity cost of various assets before making a decision. This chapter will highlight some areas where opportunities exist in the cyber world and physically in your region. We'll take a look at a few business assets and how it may be part of your overall strategy for building wealth.

Regionless Pursuit

Your own region is stocked with many opportunities. At a

minimum, besides being an employee, if you're still doing that, there must be passive income from real estate investments, brick and mortar business, online business, and dividends from paper assets such as stocks and bonds. The key is to carefully examine each area and have a clear understanding before entering that arena. No matter who you are and how much you are worth, any acquisition of assets would benefit from a system of research that enables you to evaluate opportunities.

When researching your region, do not neglect to consider regionless pursuit. I'm talking about an asset that is not affected by any region at all. A profitable business in e-commerce, for instance, will work with no regards to region. It is simply selling products and services via the internet. There's no storefront or public office. All the transactions are done online. Services are delivered digitally, and all products are shipped to the customer. Customer service issues are handled with a portal, email, or via contact us form.

This first consideration is important for so many reasons. For one, the overhead is typically lower for startups. This lower upfront cost is important to folks that are starting from the bottom. This is due to the fact that you can operate with just a laptop or smartphone wherever you find yourself. A few other things like a website and management systems are also required. However, the cost pales in comparison to brick and mortar. Very successful people like people and companies started out with this model and are now worth billions of dollars. One noticeable name is Jeff Bezos, who started his Amazon business from his garage. As you can see, where you start doesn't determine where you will end.

There's a continued growth in online sales. More and more people see the convenience that buying a product or service online brings. These rising numbers are especially so in developing regions of the Middle East and Africa. Overall, there's a steady growth of online shoppers worldwide. Like Amazon, you can always grow into brick and mortar when the time arrives for such a transition. The list of things that can be bought and sold via e-commerce is quite astonishing. A quick look at Amazon or Alibaba will surprise you. Virtually almost anything can be bought and sold on the internet.

Region Specific Opportunities

Name your region, and I can tell you dozens of viable opportunities for asset acquisition. What I wish to convey is that there's no shortage of asset creation or accumulation through purchase. Simply providing a solution to a problem for a sizeable group in your region is an asset creation and of course, there's always a willing seller of asset in every region. Identifying those that sell below the market value for their own unique reasons is one right way to accumulate asset. Another way is perhaps buying at market value but re-purposing the asset so that it generates a high rate of return. In fact, one is only limited by the failure to think creatively when it comes to asset opportunities in your region.

Nearly every opportunity that you find in your region also exists in neighbouring areas. The key is being able to identify these opportunities when you see them. The good news is that a trained way of looking at potential assets works everywhere. Learn to pinpoint profitable assets and apply this skill wherever you go.

Although a trained mind can spot asset opportunities anywhere, conditions in one region may differ significantly in another. For example, one region may be a staple manufacturing area, while another is known for its agriculture. Knowing where you choose to do business or pursue other types of asset is important. Comparing and contrasting key indicators to identify opportunities between two places gives insight into chances of success.

The food businesses like restaurants and grocery stores are areas that can thrive everywhere there are people. Everyone must eat, but where they choose to eat can be determined by quality, service, and price. Franchises usually do well in the food business because of factors such as proven systems, bulk purchase, name recognition, and some trade secrets. An investment into a carefully evaluated business like this is an asset that is sure to win. The takeaway is utilizing the proper system in determining whether the business is profitable or not. Paying for the right consulting to make this determination is an expense that's well worth it.

The plan should be elaborate to include accessory items for sale. In other words, a restaurant should have take-home refreshments, sauces, and other condiments for sale. It should also have catering services and party packages. A grocery store should be expanded to include a gas station and car wash. Also, a convenient store will serve as a surplus, but may bring in more revenues than the profits from the gas itself.

There are many other opportunities in your region. Just staying present as you roam about your daily routine can unveil lots of opportunities to inspect. Aside from food, gas, and carwash, other big areas of opportunities in your region are services.

"Opportunity is missed by most people because it is dressed in overalls and looks like work." - Thomas A. Edison

CHAPTER ELEVEN:

Global Reach through Consulting

One mistake I see investors make often is to limit themselves to investing only in their backyard. While investing locally is great, there is an ample amount of opportunities worldwide. Success outside of your area of familiarity is dependent on your ability to research, travel, and identify where potential lies. Consult with professional experts in that area to further explore your options. You may find the next big asset to acquire.

These days, global reach is just a matter of a video call and access to the internet. Using the video call technology, for instance, you can view a piece of property anywhere in real time without being there. This also makes it possible to do video conferencing with your team on the ground. It doesn't stop there as many other things can be accomplished, such as training, social proof, and verification, to name a few. Regardless of the asset type that you wish to pursue, technology has made it much easier to go global. We are going to take a birds-eye view of investment opportunities across the globe in this chapter.

Pursuit of ~~Happiness~~ Assets

Caribbean Islands & South America

When people think of the Caribbean, they think beautiful islands with great people, delicious food, and gorgeous scenery. Indeed, these are all true. By all means, do indulge as a consumer, but it's sweeter to use the cash flow proceeds from your assets. As an asset pursuer, however, you must see opportunities that others miss. Just a little research will reveal an enormous opportunity in the Caribbean and South America. Among these are commercial properties to residential, agriculture, energy, transportation, tourism, and the list goes on. Besides what's listed here, simply looking into an asset of your interest in these areas will give insight as to whether you should dig a little deeper to uncover more.

In terms of commercial properties in the Caribbean, hotels are the front runners as the tourism industry produces over $50 billion a year. That's 15% of its gross domestic product or GDP.

A large portion of this comes from hotels and its related services. South America does more at $380 billion a year, but it's also much bigger than the tiny islands of the Caribbean.

Residential units like apartment complexes in manufacturing areas or other areas of thriving economies are also in demand in many nations such as Brazil and Chile. The same holds for a major oil area like Venezuela and Trinidad/Tobago to a lesser degree. Conventional wisdom tells us that wherever there are jobs, there is a need for housing, food, energy, and transportation. Each country and island has its own flourishing economy of asset; therefore, it is important to do your own research based on your interest.

54 Countries of Africa

The original birthplace of humankind, the United States of Africa or soon to be, is home to the most mineral-rich deposits in the world. Whether it's gold, diamond, silver, copper, titanium, platinum, coal, bauxite (aluminum), uranium, oil, and a host of others, Africa has it in abundance, but not in an infinite amount. If corruption was reduced to a minimal and systems are enforced to hold competent leaders accountable, a regulated state mining industry will benefit investors and the general population. Getting this right is an asset that would benefit many more people than it currently does.

Although countries like South Africa, Nigeria, Egypt, Ghana, Ethiopia, Angola, Kenya, and many others are repositioning themselves on the right path, more can be done in the broad areas of industrialization and manufacturing. Every country is ready for it. People and institutions that are already achieving success in the so-called developed countries can duplicate the success in any of the 54 underdeveloped countries in Africa. Since the cost of living is not high, fair but, lower wages is more accepted; therefore, the profit potential should be higher.

It does not make sense to import on a large scale, the things that Africa utilize the most. At the top of the list is food. There are vast opportunities in responsible agriculture. Land cultivation and growing enough food with excess to export is an area of great potential in terms of assets.

Agriculture is said to be the largest economy in Africa, but if we had an accurate account of the minerals that are taken out of Africa each day, the masses of poor people would rebel at such robbery. After all, none is benefiting them even though many endanger their lives to mine these fortune, at compensations less than that of a slave.

As far as agriculture is concerned, there is an enormous amount of fertile land and farmers willing to cultivate it. The challenges are investment in modern technology and the elimination of unfair prices from imports outside of Africa. The locals cannot stay in business if inferior foods are brought in and sold at cheaper prices.

Investing and industrializing in food is followed by clothing. A manufacturing company that focuses on garments would thrive. Since there's always a shortage of power in Africa, investing in hydro-electric plants, solar or wind power should be explored. Frequent and unpredictable power outage called dumsor is a big problem that can be solved to end power supply outages. Residential real estate investor would benefit well by providing safe homes and apartment complexes as the population continues to increase.

Essentially opening manufacturing plants that produce cars, furniture, household supplies, technology, etc. are all areas where too much import takes place. Making the investment to grab a fair share of the market without the cost of export and tariffs would enable greater profits. The local plants would pay lower salaries and therefore generate more profits. All of these can happen by a first initiating consulting through global reach.

As I stated in the beginning, I'm all for pursuing assets. However, fair prices must be paid to the original owner. Assets must also be acquired legally and ethically without human rights violation. Failure to heed to the right way of pursuing assets will manifest itself in the form of justice when the conditions become ripe for it. The suffering people will always have the last say.

Asia

With about 4.5 billion people, Asia is home to the largest population on the planet. The people make up 60% of the world's population. Its minerals, agriculture, and services-based industries provides an ample amount of opportunities for asset pursuit. Whether it's the abundant amount of natural resources, technology manufacturing or information technology, Asia is booming, and there's more room for investors.

There are so many industries to list, but virtually any asset of interest can be tapped into on this continent. The labor cost here is also a bit cheaper as compared to that of Europe and America due to a lower cost of living in the majority of the continent. Although other places such as Hong Kong, China, Tokyo, Japan, and Singapore have a very high cost of living, the chances of greater asset brand or greater earnings are great.

"In the business world, everyone is paid in two coins: cash and experience. Take the experience first; the cash will come later." - Harold Geneen

CHAPTER TWELVE:

Wherever technology reaches

The innovations in technology assets in the past three decades have opened doors to many more advancements, and the opportunities continue to expand each year. Specifically speaking, the emergence of the internet and smartphone. So much can be done by anyone with a smartphone and a data plan. With some training and creativity, aspiring entrepreneurs can create a business right from their smartphone. These possibilities were unfounded just over a decade ago, and now it is a reality.

It is good and exciting to know about the internet and the smartphone inventions, but there's one invention that precipitated them. In fact, its own evolution has made it possible to advance the newer technologies. These developments occurred over time, but rapid innovation contributed to the overall technology we now enjoy. In this chapter, we will review the evolution of technology and how it might be used today in managing and developing assets.

Communications

Many of the technologies today would not be possible without its predecessors. While some more be stand alone, one particular invention and its innovation throughout the years have made way for how we function. The invention I speak of is telecommunications. It began around 1876 with plain old telephone service or POTS which were installed in homes and businesses. This technology asset gave way to being able to talk to people in another room or building. The distance capabilities continued to expand within a short period of time. What began as a not so clear human voice over copper wire lines in short distances eventually became clear voices citywide. Cities began to get connected, and soon it was possible to talk on the telephone, not only statewide but nationwide. As more research and testing were conducted, more improvements were made. In the progression of such developments arose transcontinental communication.

Our society's need for higher speed and bandwidth has continually been answered through lots of lab research. In fact, during the days of the POTS, which was an analog technology, additional technologies were constantly being explored. It wasn't until 1988 when integrated service digital network or ISDN, which is a digital transmission, made it possible to transmit at a much faster rate. It also made the transmission of voice and data on the same line possible. Since then and over a few decades, telecommunications technology has reach light speeds. It is important to understand this as I make the correlation across several occurrences.

We've come a long way from twisted copper lines communication through POTS to ISDN, then later digital subscriber line or DSL and now high-speed fiber optic systems. When the World Wide Web was invented in 1990 and began to gain grounds, the amount of average data transmitted over the internet was minuscule, yet it was very slow. It is also worth noting that networks, in general, existed prior to 1983 but the mother of them all, sometimes called the network of networks, or the internet project didn't begin until then. The World Wide Web, however, became the most common way of accessing data on the internet. Thanks to DSL, communications over the internet became much faster even though the data being sent and received grew. Today, due to bandwidth technology, precision data transmission, as well as audio and video, are now transmitted faster than imaginable. More inventions based on communications awaits this generation as well as the future ones. The next asset that derives from this technology could be as big as Amazon or other massive technology-dependent company.

Data Mining

One of the challenges of having abundant data all over the internet is how to examine it quickly and effectively in order to generate new useful information. The solution is a technology called data mining. It is a process of examining database systems, including machine learning and statistics. Through data mining, patterns are discovered, and the analysis is used to solve future problems. Among these are future trends and forecasting. Important stages include exploration, modeling, and deployment. Data mining is an asset that benefits businesses of all types and areas because it enables higher efficiency. Those that use it will excel noticeably than those that remain oblivious to it.

Being able to uncover hidden information or patterns gives an edge that adds value to all assets, and therefore, its impact cannot be ignored.

The outcome of data mining can be used to improve customer relations and ultimately increase future revenues. The potential is enormous as more and more use for data mining continues to be explored. One of the areas all businesses are concerned with is how to cut cost. Techniques in data mining can help accomplish this, and much more as many industries are able to analyze pertinent information to help their bottom line quickly.

With so much information all over the web and its continual growth, having the ability to dig through it and find data that will help your business is essential. There's no way this can be accomplished manually, so artificial intelligence and machine learning makes sense in predicting future trends. Big retailers, financial institutions, banking, manufacturing, telecommunication, and education are just a few industries that are using data mining as assets to make advances and increase their profits. Data mining is still young, so the potential to capitalize on this asset is as wide as your creativity.

Cloud Computing

Once upon a time, not long ago, companies had to purchase, configure, and manage their computer systems as well as digital storage systems. As they grow and the need for more computing or storage arose, the process had to be repeated over and over again. Those that have servers needed a solution as well because when their systems fail or become defective, replacing them was also quite a challenge in terms of cost, human resource, time, and risk of possible downtime if redundancy of their systems is affected. The overall installation, repair, and maintenance of computing systems of especially large organizations needed a better way. It needed a powerful, cost-effective option to operate while having the ability to scale up quickly without a glitch. The answer is cloud computing.

Cloud computing is a solution that solves all the challenges mentioned above. It is the ability to do virtually all your computing and digital storage through a host, thereby not having to purchase or service your own equipment. The computing services ability such as databases, software, networking, and a host of others all made possible by remote servers over the internet. Customers can purchase these services, and increase or decrease usage as needed, which also means price adjustments. With cloud technology, you simply pay for what you use.

Besides lowering operating cost, cloud computing is an asset that offers superior security, speed, productivity, scalability, and performance. It is called cloud computing, but in essence, it is a cluster of physical remote servers that makes it all possible. It can be operated by a third-party cloud provider, private provider, or a combination of both. Its main categories are IaaS or infrastructure as a service, PaaS or platform as a service and SaaS or software as a service. There's also server-less computing that enables the functionality of building apps without a server.

With cloud computing, a start-up app company, for instance, can begin operations at a low cost and do it quickly on a pay as you go bases. This changes the game because the capital needed to get started is also reduced dramatically. Apart from that, there are other advantages, such as scaling up or down in just a few minutes, and no maintenance cost. This is an asset users can use to deliver software on demand, store data, create apps, stream audio/video, build and test applications, among others. Your success is waiting on your creativity with this technology.

Large companies such as Microsoft, Amazon, and AT&T offer cloud services for the public as well as using it themselves. Currently, Amazon web services is the largest provider of cloud computing as they have more than 50% of the market, while all the other providers have the remaining 50% together. The cloud is here to stay, and the opportunities surrounding it are enormous in terms of what assets can be generated from it. Just think, if you can build the next app company such as Uber, Facebook, Skype, Google, Instagram, WhatsApp, YouTube, Snapchat, Udemy, TED, Mint, Acorns, Airbnb, Xender, and Lyft, etc. Now imagine having the ability to build a company of the named caliper, right from your laptop.

"The science of today is the technology of tomorrow".
Edward Teller

SECTION V

Asset Power Moves: Who and How?

It all starts with a dream powered by your ambition. Leadership transcends your vision to key partners and ultimately, your team and affiliates. Knowing who to add to your team is of great importance. If you plan on having a sizable asset, you'll need to formulate a group of competent and experienced people who respect your leadership and not only understand but subscribe to your overall vision.

There is a necessity of forming an alliance of key partners of mutual benefits to assist in various aspects of your asset pursuit. If you don't select this people carefully based on track record, you could find yourself spinning your wheels as opposed to making progress. Highly effective people with integrity are indispensable and you must sort and attain them.

In these final chapters, we'll analyze who to include and how to screen team members in your asset pursuit. It's about choices. Team formulation that will benefit you from leadership to other key partner's selection are all outlined here. Even those that are affiliated to you must be carefully chosen to ensure quality to your brand, and not tarnish it.

CHAPTER THIRTEEN:

Leadership

When it comes to leadership asset, all sizes are not created equal. The skill level required to be a leader differs based on the magnitude of the ventures and overall goal. Still, there's a level of skill that all leaders must possess. Strategies have to be executed to accomplish objectives, but before all of that occurs, there must be leadership. Without it, businesses and institutions will remain stagnant or even collapse. Leadership is the ability to see beyond what meets the eye. It's about seeing with the mind, a vision that others may not have imagined. The leadership presents a realistic agenda of what must be accomplished in the future and timeframe as it relates to the organization. Strategies to do it can be delegated to management who works under the leadership. We'll cover managers at greater details in chapter 15 as they are the keys to accomplishing priorities. For this chapter, we'll focus on the leader or CEO. The one who sets the agenda we call the vision, what it entails, and the mission to be performed daily.

The Leader

A leader is a person who is charged with the responsibility or assumes the top spot of an organization. If title matters, this leader would be the chief executive officer or CEO. He or She leads or command a group; therefore, communications skills is essential for this person. The leader who deems themselves effective based on measurement must be inspiring and analytical. His or her vision has to be calculated and convincing. It is necessary that a leader motivates the team. In the pursuit of assets, a leader is all about the assets. Everything that entails the assets survival, growth, and profit is the responsibility of the leader.

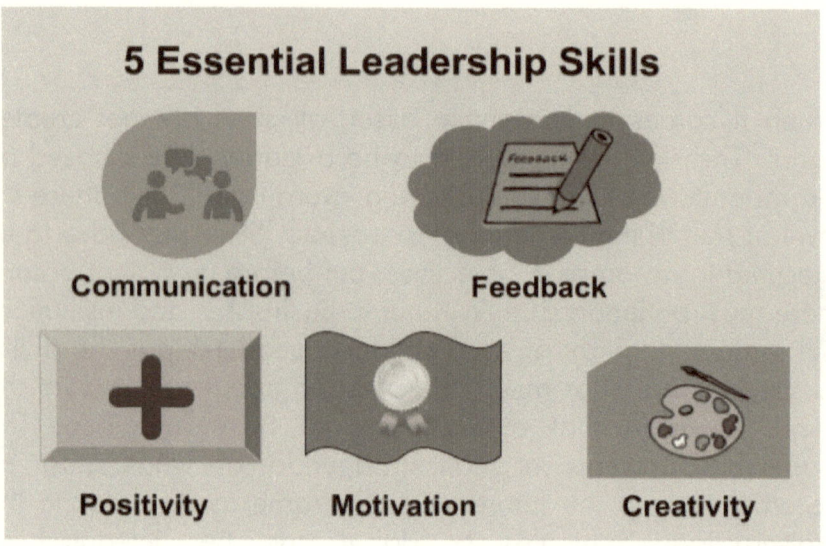

In essence, the leader constantly works on the outside perimeter of the assets. He or she sets agenda with confidence, so the team is eager to follow. No one wants to follow a leader that lacks honesty, passion, and integrity. However, nearly everyone likes accountability and decisiveness. An effective leader or head of an institution makes major decisions for managers to plan and execute. The ability to forecast is essential for any leader that wishes for their company to remain relevant.

I added this segment after the book was completed to illustrate an example of leadership for creating this book. I had a vision to repurpose some of my expertise in creating wealth for the masses. Although I have online courses to help people, I felt a book would serve as an accessible reference. Besides, I know the power and value of good books. This is not my first book, so planning was as smooth. As a leader, I activated my team. I informed my team of the project and the inspiration behind it. I wanted to educate people about assets. The vision was to capture systematically the answers to the 5 W's and the H. I told them when completed; a reader should feel inspired to pursue assets at any level.

The plan included an outline of the book including cosmetics such as book cover etc., research topics, manuscript, editing, formatting, targeted date of completion, publishing, distribution, marketing, and assigned responsibilities of the team. My responsibility as a leader was to write the manuscript and have various members of the team execute their duties to bring the book into existence. The asset is the book. Therefore, it was the center of my focus. With my team inspired and motivated, all I had to do was produce the very best material and let them put it all together. For months, I worked on the content, and my team discharged their duties mentioned above. In the end, we rolled out this must-read book for people who wants to build wealth.

The takeaway is that I had an idea that became a vision. I provided leadership and set the agenda. Everyone understood what we intended to accomplish. The outline of the project, its inspiration, and the benefits it stands to serve motivated my team. A clear vision was stated, and all members knew their roles in the overall project. They also embraced the mission of what and when duties needed to be completed. I created the content, and my team assembled the other components to bring forth the publication. During the project, I acted as a project manager, ensuring that we were all on track. To realize success, everyone needed to perform their task to meet our target. In the end, what began as an idea is now a book called the pursuit of assets.

The Vision

The direction in terms of vision is provided by the leader. It tells a story of where an organization is headed. The future of a company should be captured in its vision. A clear vision makes it easy for the team to understand the purpose and long-term game plan. A managers' job is a bit easier when the leader's vision is clear and concise. It's about what needs to be done in the near future.

Every vision is made public byway of a vision statement. Although a leader's vision can be verbalized, it is standard to communicate it in writing as well for the record. It is designed to inspire and give a sense of direction to where a company sees itself going forward. It picks up from where you are and stipulate where you should be. Making it easy for the entire team to understand the vision is important because they are the ones who produce daily contributions towards it.

The Mission

The mission is different in that it deals with what's happening now. Present activity is what mission is all about. It's like an advertisement, so it covers the purpose with built-in policies to achieve it. The team must find the mission engaging in order to attain success, so having a good manager is an asset to the mission. It must be clear and easy to follow, but most of all, it must be something that can be done now.

Mission statements exist to inform team members and the public of the purpose of the organization's existence. When you read a mission statement, you should understand what its company does, who their targets are, and where they're located. It is even more important to know how to do it. This is the job of a manager, and it will be covered in chapter 15. The mission should reflect your asset and declare what it is and the value it brings.

"Don't find fault, find remedy." Henry Ford

CHAPTER FOURTEEN:

Experienced Key Partners

The mistake of trying to take a cheaper route in terms of key partners when it comes to assets is more costly than paying competitive prices for top producers. I repeat, only select the best of the best as key partners. They are the best in their respective fields for a reason. When you neglect this notion, often at times, you are left with frustration and redo's when it could have been avoided in the first place. It is important to emphasize because an experienced professional who sits at the top of his/ her industry gets results. When you want success, you have to team up with key partners of such caliper to forward your agenda.

This chapter is dedicated to showing the importance of experienced key partners not only in real estate but assets as a whole.

There are a few indispensable people that should be in your circle. Having them will add value to your assets. Selecting the best of the best is the subject to be covered here.

Real Estate Broker/Agent

Let's take buying a real estate property for an example. Working with the best brokers/agents means fast access and closing with connections to top lenders, title companies, inspectors, appraisers, insurance agencies, and contractors. The entire experience is sure to move swiftly with minimum issues that could delay the process. Do you see the value? Acquiring a property is already a lengthy process that can take 30 to 60 days if lending is involved, so why take a chance with a mediocre real estate broker/agent? They could cause delays and frustrations, so avoid them even if the commission is cheaper. Time is money, an asset that should be valued. By working with the best, you can finish deals faster and pursue other deals.

The real estate broker and or agent handles all the contract documents. These contracts can be overwhelming, especially on larger acquisitions. With an experienced top broker/agent, your best interest is protected. Most of these professionals have links to top real estate attorneys as well. If you are not sure about any portion of the contract, you can use their review or take it to your own real estate attorney. Top professional has the staff support and systems necessary to provide a great experience one transaction at a time.

Corporate Attorney

The purpose of a corporate attorney is the ongoing counsel and legal advice you will get so you can stay abreast of current rules, regulations, policies, changes, and best practices, etc. They will draw, negotiate, and interpret contracts on your behalf. When you have an attorney on your team, they'll help you with compliance issues. You will avoid many unforeseen problems from occurring while having the confidence that future legal issues will be handled by a competent person who you trust.

One of the first things when planning on your asset pursuit would be to sit with a reputable attorney, who specializes in asset protection and estate planning that governs the home of your institutions. The consultation should address all your assets. It should also cover how to best protect your assets from theft, lawsuits, probate, and excessive tax. Lastly, anything that you may not have thought about would probably be covered as well. Specialize attorney in the field of asset protection knows how to best protect everything you and your organizations own.

Most people know about personal identity theft, but there's also business identity theft. Protect yourself and your entities against both. Thieves look for weak or poorly protected people and businesses to target. When this occurs, a large quantity of money can be stolen. Business credit and products can be ordered and invoiced in the victim or its company's name. You must guard against these potential illegal activities, so it never happens to you. Protection at times also serves as a deterrent against such vultures.

It seems a lot of people want the smallest opportunity to sue a prosperous company. These days, issues that can easily be resolved outside of litigation are taken to court in hopes of winning a substantial judgment. Avoid being the defendant in such cases by protecting your assets. Taking measures to protect yourself properly means that you become more untouchable than many others. If your assets have layers of protection, it makes it difficult for attorneys to go after you.

They want cases that are seen as easy to win and a substantial amount to gain. When a would-be plaintiff consults with an attorney, that attorney will conduct an asset search. They do this primarily to decide whether to take the case or not, especially if being paid is contingent on winning the case. Asset searches can reveal a lot, and if they found assets that are not protected

Pursuit of ~~Happiness~~ Assets

correctly, they will go after it. If documents are not properly filed, etc., the courts can pierce the corporate veil and regard you and your entity as one. This means they can go after all your assets, including your personal assets. A corporate attorney will help you protect your assets.

Business & Tax Accountant

An accountant on your team means complicated tax code and number crunching is a non-issue. They can get things done much quicker, professionally, and with less scrutiny from the IRS. Your accountant should perform services such as calculating your assets, equity, and liability. They should file all necessary local state and federal income tax. Even with an accountant, it is still important that you stay organize and maintain a book of all business-related transactions.

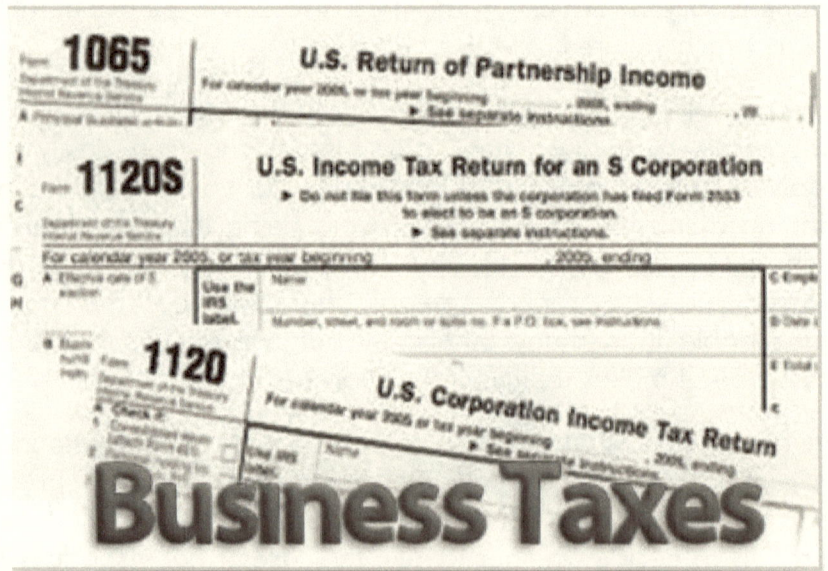

In fact, being organized helps your accountant perform their duties more efficiently. A good accountant will give clients a format to follow in record keeping. It helps both parties and makes finding documents in the future very easy. An accountant stays abreast of all changes and regulation. When you have a tax accountant on your team, you can focus on more important tasks like expanding or acquiring more assets.

Other Key Partners

The mere intention of pursuing real estate assets means you should equip yourself with a couple of high performing real estate agents. My philosophy is to partner with the best in your ventures as they'll save you time, money, and maybe even frustration. For starters, real estate agents have access to the multiple listing service or MLS, which is a marketing database by real estate brokers. This database is made available online by each local association, and its purpose is to list properties for sale or rent. Along with the listing comes pertinent tools such as sales and rent comparable. These comps, as it is shortened, allow potential sellers and buyers to see the market rate for properties based on size, type, and proximity of properties. With an agent at your disposal, you can get a hold of the information quickly so you can analyze and make decisions faster.

Real estate agents can also handle the contracts involved in selling and buying a property and most importantly list your property for sale in the MLS for a seller and show listing for a buyer. These agents do have a fee of 6% for most cases to list and sell your property and may split the money with the buyer's agent.

Unless you plan on financing your own asset purchases, you'll need loan officers and private money lenders. These people can be the difference between acquiring an asset or missing out on one. Having a relationship with these professionals' means, they know your credit history and ability to pay your debt as well as your net worth and what assets you currently own. Lending can be made available much faster when you have a lender in your corner.

"THE ROAD TO SUCCESS AND THE ROAD TO FAILURE ARE ALMOST EXACTLY THE SAME." - Colin R. Davis

CHAPTER FIFTEEN:

A Team That Embodies Your Vision

Everything in terms of business assets starts at the top. A leader has to assemble a team that not only believes in the vision but embodies it. Although the leader sets the agenda, it is the managers that carries it out. This is why it's extremely important to have a clear vision and mission when you are a leader of any group.

In this final chapter, our focus will be on the team. The team you assemble is a reflection of the success you aim to achieve. Managers, workforce, and affiliates that makes up a great team are explored. You'll learn how to screen and select these professionals to embody your vision.

Managers

Manager are the ones who plans and executes the overall agenda. They work closely with the leadership to make sure targets and timeframe are understood. The daily operations is a function of a manager. He or she is an extension of a chief executive officer or CEO, the highest-ranking member of an organization. A manager is responsible for quality and customer service. They recruit, train, and ensure employees know and follow company policies and standards. Whether its financial objectives or establishing strategic goals, a manager should be equipped to do it all.

A good manager is very valuable to a company, and every effort should be made to get one. It could be the difference between a well-run institution and one that struggles. Other qualities invaluable to an institution is the ability to get results and endure pressure. As part of the leadership, a manager is all about providing clear performance expectation as well as improvement strategies. When there's a new task to be accomplished, it is up to a manager to motivate the staff. Communications, interpersonal, and decision-making skills are vital to a manager.

A key asset to any company, a qualified manager not only assembles the best people, he or she also brings out the best in them. This can be accomplished through a skillful use of speaking, writing, time management, analytics, and problem resolution. Rewarding and disciplining employees as needed is just two of the many duties performed at this position. A manager does training, evaluations of productivity, and much more to meet the bottom line.

The Workforce

A team that embodies a leaders' vision is not complete without the workforce. These are the folks that produce for the benefit of your assets. They report directly to a manager who should know how to hire the best talents, perform background check, credit check, and routine drug check if applicable. Look for talents that are suitable for the type of business you are establishing. Hire the best and make sure you do not discriminate based on race, gender, nationality, disability, or others outlined by the Equal Employment Opportunity Commission or its equivalent in your country. Operating policies should dictate that managers follow labor laws by hiring people that are age appropriate and legally permissible to work in your country. Be sure to pay above minimum wage as you will get more out of your team if you give them incentives to do more. Higher wages can be paid when you produce superior quality, and such product or services are possible with higher compensations for your workforce.

References are a must, so do ask each employee candidate for three professional references and three personal. Expect the personal ones to sing their praises. The professional references, on the other hand, tend to be more upfront about their experience with your candidates. Follow the law on what you can and cannot ask them as you conduct your reference checks. Simply introduce yourself and ask if the manager can talk for a few minutes.

Proceed to tell them the reason for the call. Use your own style but be sure to start by asking if they know your candidate. Ask them their relationship with your candidate and what job duties the candidate performed. Finish your inquiry by asking if the candidate qualifies for re-hire. When an employer says no to that question, it is a clear signal that should not be taken lightly.

This is a screening process to see which candidates should receive further consideration. Those that get passed this stage can now be scheduled for a formal interview. There is no need to waste time doing interviews unless you can learn a few things about your potential employee. Screening your applicants like this will save both parties an enormous amount of time and cease any false hopes.

During the interview, ask questions that are designed to have insight into who there are and look for consistency and good work ethics. Attendance is always a big issue, so dig deep to ensure that your applicants don't have a serious problem with attendance. Make sure the people selected are able to work as scheduled and execute their duties with little or no supervision.

The manager should select employees and leave a few on a reserve list and set time for training and orientation. During this period, cover the company's policies for operating, safety, emergency, attendance, lock-down, customer service, and others. Be sure to have employees complete all necessary forms such as tax forms, employment eligibility forms, and other industry-specific forms. In fact, it is good to keep a master checklist to make sure all items are covered. You must have a salary or wage agreement that includes job title and description, frequency, and method of payment. Have a dress code, so your brand remains consistent. Ensure that your entire staff knows the chain of command.

Employers have federal insurance contribution act or FICA tax responsibilities. Your tax accountant can bring you up to speed on current rates and requirements. Although employees pay social security and Medicare, you as the employer must match it. In other words, you will match the current rate of 6.2 percent of social security tax and 1.45 percent of Medicare tax for a total of 12.4 and 2.9 percent at the time of this publication. These percentages are important as they are part of your payroll expenses. Having just a few employees keeps payroll cost down.

An employer has no cost in federal income tax but is responsible for deducting it and sending it to the internal revenue service or IRS via form 941 every quarter. Form 1099 should be provided to contractors or anyone you pay that is not a regular employee.

Affiliates

Affiliates are an asset to any company. These folks are not employees nor contractors. Their duty is to promote your products or services for a fee. I am a big fan of affiliates because they can take a business to a new level in terms of sales. Affiliates are a marketing machine without the cost of marketing. Any business asset can benefit from affiliate marketing as it's designed to pay only a portion of the profit proceeds.

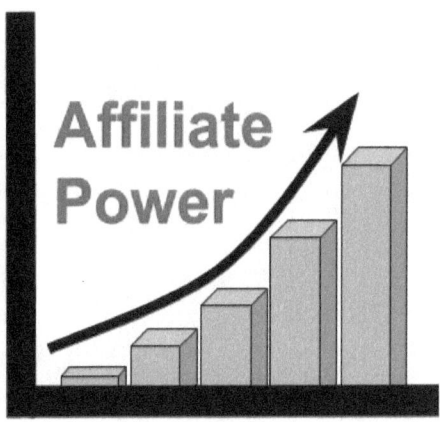

To fully understand what affiliates can do for your business, imagine having one thousand new customers a month. Give these customers an incentive to promote your business. If 50% of these people bring you one customer each, you'll have one thousand five hundred new customers. This pattern will continue to replicate itself. The profits are guaranteed before it is shared.

On the other hand, money spent on traditional marketing has no guarantees, only an estimate. With affiliate marketing, it cost you the employer nothing until you make a profit. Having an unlimited amount of people working to promote your assets is essential for maximizing profits.

"Teamwork is the ability to work together toward a common vision. The ability to direct individual accomplishments toward organizational objectives. It is the fuel that allows common people to attain uncommon results." - ANDREW CARNEGIE

CONCLUSION

It appears that making the decision to pursue assets does not come easy for some people. Among the reasons people give are not knowing how to do it, and where to get help. These top two explanations tend to hold many back from pursuing an abundant life of wealth. If there's a burning desire and that desire yields to nothing, the outcome is likely to be an achievement of extraordinary proportions. Now, it may seem like it's a no-brainer, but many never make that decision. Many live their lives as though a miracle will just appear one day and make them wealthy. Unfortunately, that is not reality.

It is up to you to make a decision when it comes to having the confidence needed to believe you can achieve success in building wealth. It's not magic because magic is an illusion. Wealth is merely an idea and a process that requires action for success. Although people may say they want wealth, many say it without conviction. It appears to be casual and not supported with any real pledge. This phenomenon may be a result of self-doubt. Some of the reasons for not deciding to pursue assets includes not thinking it can happen, not knowing what to do to attain it, and not having the resources.

There has to be a mindset shift because this way of thinking has been indoctrinated into us since we were children. The sentiment was to get educated the traditional way through our school systems. Upon graduation, secure a good job, and begin to consume material things. Since most people fall for this type of lifestyle, they echo this narrative to their loved ones. As a result, many young folk graduate college with large student debt. They then compound more debt by accumulating material wishes of their desire.

Choose a different path and start learning about personal finance. Make it a priority to know the difference between asset and liability truly. If you choose assets, your understanding will lead you to take action. Sort out a mentor or a coach. This will be someone that has a proven record of successfully doing what you're trying to do. I can certainly be your mentor and coach you. I get excited when people take action and actually start to implement my systems of wealth building for themselves. You can reach me on social media, my website, or simply email me at repak7@gmail.com. Join my Facebook group. It is called Devise Wealth Mastermind. I'm there along with many other like-minded people that can help you figure it all out.

Your pursuit and attainment of assets involve the cooperation and assistance of others. Therefore, it is meaningless unless you give back in an impactful manner. Display leadership skills, hire a competent, experienced, and dedicated team with fair compensation. Providing additional pay incentives or benefit will serve as a motivator for the team and ultimately help you reach your goals. Be decisive, kind, and generous; however, do not waver from your own policies as that will signal team members to do the same.

The pursuit of assets can and should commence now. It can start as small as feasible with built-in growth plans. No goal of acquiring assets is too small or too big. The level you reach and attain is dependent on your efforts, access to capital, your team, and the ability to leverage what you have to get what you want. It is a long-term plan but checking milestones along the way will ensure you stay on course. Happiness cannot buy anything of value, or be transferred to your loved ones, but assets can. The correct agenda is the pursuit of assets.

Pursuit of ~~Happiness~~ Assets

Other Publications & Educational Materials by the Author

BOOKS

Little Money Big Credit

5 Principles for Becoming Wealthy

Nurture

ONLINE COURSES AT
Academy.Devisewealth.Com

Debt Elimination

Pay Off Your House in 5 Years

Establish and Maintain Great Credit

Save Short-term Money for Assets

How to Build Wealth Forever

BLOGS AT *Devisewealth.com*

5 Reasons why many People are not Rich

Becoming Wealthy from The bottom up

Steps for Great Credit *and much more!*

Kenneth Botwe

TRAINING VIDEOS AT
YouTube.com/user/KennethBotwe

First thing you must do to Become Wealthy

Payoff your House in 5 Years

How to get out of Debt *and much more!*

www.ingramcontent.com/pod-product-compliance
Lightning Source LLC
Chambersburg PA
CBHW032017170526
45157CB00002B/735